MathFlare

Name: ________________________

Class: __________

Teacher: ________________________

AF483820

Introduction

As parents and educators, we recognize the pivotal role mathematics plays in shaping a child's academic journey and future success. Yet, the path to mathematical proficiency can often seem daunting, fraught with challenges and complexities. That's where the transformative power of MathFlare Workbooks shine through, illuminating the way forward with clarity, precision, and purpose.

Introducing MathFlare Workbooks – a beacon of guidance, a testament to excellence, and a catalyst for achievement. Crafted with meticulous care and expertise, MathFlare Workbooks stand as paragons of educational excellence, designed to nurture young minds, ignite a passion for learning, and develop a deep-rooted understanding of mathematical concepts.

Picture this: your child eagerly delves into the pages of Mathflare Workbook, greeted by a step-by-step guide illuminated with vivid examples that demystify complex mathematical concepts. With each turn of the page, they embark on a journey of discovery, encountering thoughtfully curated practice questions that reinforce learning and hone problem-solving skills. And when they unveil the answers to those very questions, a sense of accomplishment blossoms within them – a tangible reward for their hard work and dedication.

But MathFlare Workbooks are more than just tools for learning; they are pathways to comprehension, fostering a deep-seated understanding of mathematical concepts through a sequential, logical flow. From fundamental principles to advanced problem-solving strategies, every chapter builds upon the last, ensuring a robust foundation upon which future knowledge can be constructed.

As parents, we yearn for nothing more than to see our children thrive, to witness the spark of inspiration ignited within them as they conquer academic challenges with confidence and poise. MathFlare Workbooks serve as partners in this noble endeavor, offering not just practice questions, but the keys to unlocking a world of opportunity.

And for teachers, MathFlare Workbooks stand as invaluable allies in the quest to cultivate mathematical proficiency in the classroom. With answers readily available, instructors can focus on guiding and nurturing their students, confident in the knowledge that MathFlare Workbooks provide a solid framework upon which to build.

In the pages of MathFlare Workbooks, we find not just the promise of academic excellence, but the seeds of a brighter tomorrow. So let us embrace the power of mathematics, let us champion the journey of learning, and let us pave the way for a generation of young minds poised to shape the world. With MathFlare Workbooks as our guide, the possibilities are infinite, and the future, bright.

Table of Contents

MathFlare
Grade 2
MATH WORKBOOK
Step by Step Guide and Essential Practice with Answers
Addition Subtraction
Multiplication
Place Value and Expanded Notations
Geometry
MathFlare Publishing

MathFlare
Grade 2-3
MATH WORKBOOK
Step by Step Guide and Essential Practice with Answers
Addition Subtraction
Multiplication and Division
Place Value and Expanded Notations
Geometry
MathFlare Publishing

MathFlare
Grade 3
MATH WORKBOOK
Step by Step Guide and Essential Practice with Answers
Multiplication and Division
Decimals
Place Value and Expanded Notations
Fractions and Geometry
MathFlare Publishing

MathFlare
Grade 1
MATH WORKBOOK
Step by Step Guide and Essential Practice with Answers
Counting and Numbers
Addition and Subtraction
Place Value and Expanded Notations
Understanding Time
MathFlare Publishing

MathFlare
Grade 1-2
MATH WORKBOOK
Step by Step Guide and Essential Practice with Answers
Counting and Numbers
Addition and Subtraction
Place Value and Expanded Notations
Understanding Time
MathFlare Publishing

MathFlare
Grade 3-4
MATH WORKBOOK
Step by Step Guide and Essential Practice with Answers
Addition Subtraction
Multiplication Division
Place Value and Expanded Notations
Fractions and Geometry
MathFlare Publishing

MathFlare
Grade 4
MATH WORKBOOK
Step by Step Guide and Essential Practice with Answers
Addition Subtraction
Multiplication Division
Place Value and Expanded Notations
Fractions and Geometry
MathFlare Publishing

MathFlare
Grade 4-5
MATH WORKBOOK
Step by Step Guide and Essential Practice with Answers
Multiplication Division
Place Value and Expanded Notations
Fractions and Geometry
Unit Conversion
MathFlare Publishing

MathFlare
MATH
WORKBOOK
5
Step by Step Guide
and Essential Practice
with Answers
Multiplication
Division
Place Value and
Expanded
Notations
Fractions
and Geometry
Unit
Conversion
MathFlare Publishing

MathFlare
MATH
WORKBOOK
5-6
Step by Step Guide
and Essential Practice
with Answers
Multiplication
Division
Place Value and
Expanded
Notations
Fractions
and Geometry
Units and
Statistics
MathFlare Publishing

MathFlare
MATH
WORKBOOK
6
Step by Step Guide
and Essential Practice
with Answers
Integers and
Statistics
Arithmetic and
Pre-Algebra
Fractions
and Geometry
Ratio and
Percentage
MathFlare Publishing

MathFlare
MATH
WORKBOOK
6-7
Step by Step Guide
and Essential Practice
with Answers
Arithmetic and
Pre-Algebra
Ratio, Percent
Proportion
Geometry
Statistics
MathFlare Publishing

MathFlare
MATH
WORKBOOK
7
Step by Step Guide
and Essential Practice
with Answers
Pre-Algebra
Ratio, Percent
Proportion
Geometry
Statistics
MathFlare Publishing

MathFlare
MATH
WORKBOOK
7-8
Step by Step Guide
and Essential Practice
with Answers
Pre-Algebra
Ratio, Percent
Proportion
Geometry and
Cartesian Plane
Statistics
MathFlare Publishing

MathFlare
MATH
WORKBOOK
8-9
Step by Step Guide
and Essential Practice
with Answers
Pre-Algebra
Ratio, Proportion
and Percentage
Linear
Equations
Geometry and
Cartesian Plane
MathFlare Publishing

MathFlare
MATH
WORKBOOK
8
Step by Step Guide
and Essential Practice
with Answers
Pre-Algebra
Percentage
Linear
Equations
Geometry
MathFlare Publishing

Decimals

Adding Decimals

Adding decimals is like adding whole numbers, but we must align the decimal points carefully. For instance, when adding 49.88 and 45.78:

Step 1: Align the decimal points.

$$49.88$$
$$+\ 45.78$$

Step 2: Start adding from the rightmost digit (the ones place) and move to the left.

Add 8 and 8: 8 + 8 = 16. Write down 6 in the ones place and carry over 1 to the tenths place.

$$49.88$$
$$+\ 45.78$$
$$6$$

Step 3: Add the tenths place.

Add 1 (carried over from the previous step), 8, and 7: 1 + 8 + 7 = 16. Write down 6 in the tenths place and carry over 1 to the hundredths place.

$$49.88$$
$$+\ 45.78$$
$$66$$

Step 4: Continue adding digits to the left until you reach the leftmost digit:

$$49.88$$
$$+\ 45.78$$
$$9566$$

 Finally, write the sum with the decimal point directly below the decimal points in the original numbers.

$$
\begin{array}{r}
49.88 \\
+\ 45.78 \\
\hline
95.66
\end{array}
$$

Subtracting Decimals

Subtracting decimals follows a process like adding decimals, except instead of adding the numbers, we subtract them.

Let's solve more problems:

$$
\begin{array}{r}
467.52 \\
+\ 758.37 \\
\hline
1{,}225.89
\end{array}
\qquad
\begin{array}{r}
409.71 \\
-\ 291.47 \\
\hline
118.24
\end{array}
$$

Fractions

Fractions represent parts of a whole. They consist of a numerator (the number on top) and a denominator (the number on the bottom).

For example: we have an orange, and we divide it into 5 equal slices. Each slice represents $\frac{1}{5}$ of the orange. Now, if we take 3 of those slices, we have taken $\frac{3}{5}$ of the orange.

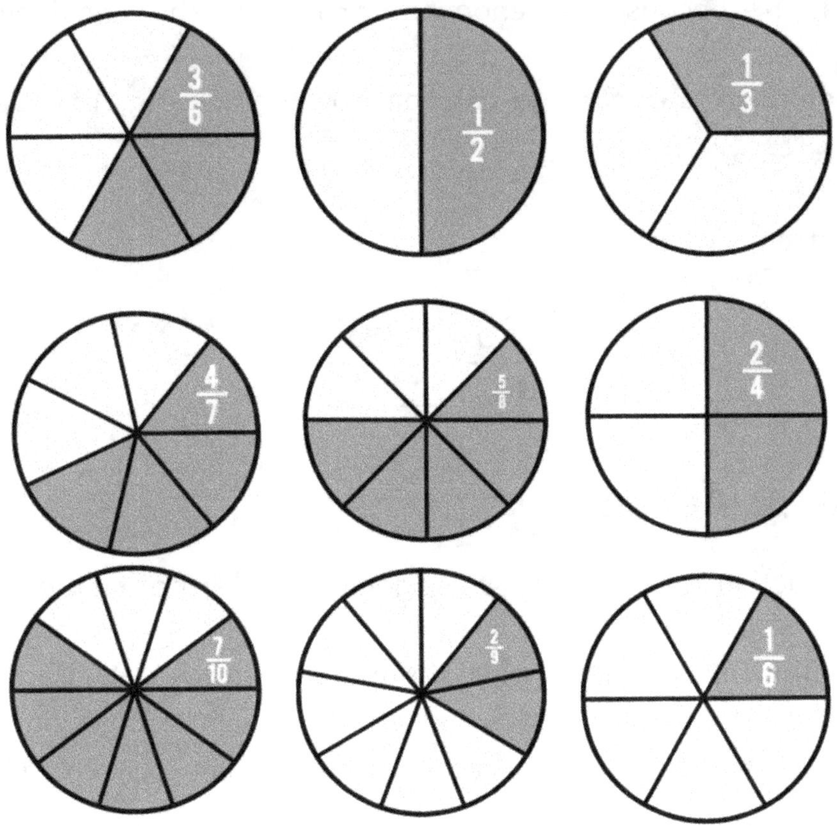

<u>Let's solve a problem:</u>

$$\square\square\square\square\square\square\,\square\square = \dfrac{5}{9}$$

Comparing Fractions

When comparing fractions, we consider the size of their denominators. Generally, the larger the denominator, the smaller the fraction.

For example:

$\frac{1}{3}$ is smaller than $\frac{1}{2}$ because the denominator 3 is larger than the denominator 2.

If the denominators are the same, we can compare the numerators to determine which fraction is larger.

Let's solve a problem:

$$\dfrac{56}{60} \underset{\underline{\quad}}{<} \dfrac{57}{60}$$

Convert Fractions to Decimals

To transform a fraction into a decimal, we divide the numerator by the denominator.

For instance, $\frac{1}{4}$ equals 0.25 because when we divide 1 by 4, we get 0.25.

In certain cases, the resulting decimal repeats infinitely, like $\frac{1}{3}$, which equals 0.3333... In such instances, we round the decimal to a specific number of decimal places.

Let's solve a problem:

$$\dfrac{52}{100} = 0.52$$

Fractions Addition (Common Denominator)

To add fractions with a common denominator, we add their numerators together and keep the denominator the same.

For example: if we want to add $\frac{3}{5}$ and $\frac{2}{5}$ both fractions have the same denominator of 5.

Therefore, to add them, we simply add their numerators:

$$\frac{3}{5} + \frac{2}{5} = \frac{3 + 2}{5} = \frac{5}{5}$$

Let's solve a problem:

$$\frac{9}{17} + \frac{1}{17} = \frac{9 + 1}{17} = \frac{10}{17}$$

Fractions Subtraction (Common Denominator)

To subtract fractions with a common denominator, we find the difference between their numerators and keep the denominator the same.

For example:

$$\frac{3}{5} - \frac{2}{5} = \frac{3 - 2}{5} = \frac{1}{5}$$

Let's solve a problem:

$$\frac{15}{16} - \frac{12}{16} = \frac{15 - 12}{16} = \frac{3}{16}$$

Fractions Multiplication

To multiply fractions, we simply multiply the numerators together to get the new numerator and multiply the denominators together to get the new denominator.

For example, let's multiply: $\dfrac{2}{4} \times \dfrac{1}{4}$

Numerator: 2 × 1 = 2

Denominator: 4 × 4 = 16

Therefore, $\dfrac{2}{16}$

we can simplify the resulting fraction:

$$\frac{1}{8}$$

Let's solve a problem:

$$\frac{4}{5} \times \frac{4}{5} = \frac{4 \times 4}{5 \times 5} = \frac{16}{25}$$

Fractions Division

To divide fractions, we multiply by the reciprocal of the divisor.

For example, let's divide:

$$\frac{6}{8} \div \frac{4}{8}$$

$$\frac{6}{8} \times \frac{8}{4} = \frac{48}{32} = \frac{3}{2}$$

Adding Decimals

Find the sum.

1.   861.36
   + 529.39

2.   789.94
   + 592.83

3.   773.22
   + 723.30

4.   306.69
   + 722.79

5.   714.24
   + 336.91

6.   858.63
   + 194.60

7.   115.73
   + 815.06

8.   731.78
   + 143.60

9.   114.17
   + 577.55

10.   125.50
   + 392.49

11.   756.38
   + 579.03

12.   406.93
   + 973.10

13.   958.58
   + 132.19

14.   320.21
   + 770.74

15.   987.28
   + 764.41

16.   455.78
   + 997.60

17.   400.71
   + 369.20

18.   808.76
   + 668.58

19.   465.59
   + 942.46

20.   560.14
   + 479.06

21.	442.91 + 335.43	22.	229.36 + 148.38	23.	573.43 + 930.01	24.	400.34 + 931.51
25.	253.50 + 560.30	26.	244.21 + 315.30	27.	760.21 + 135.13	28.	720.95 + 382.32
29.	222.46 + 816.82	30.	634.24 + 741.03	31.	503.09 + 535.94	32.	735.50 + 949.82
33.	881.11 + 861.01	34.	793.88 + 746.52	35.	106.30 + 163.20	36.	677.99 + 171.70
37.	117.40 + 646.42	38.	949.58 + 520.94	39.	449.68 + 358.55	40.	499.67 + 128.57

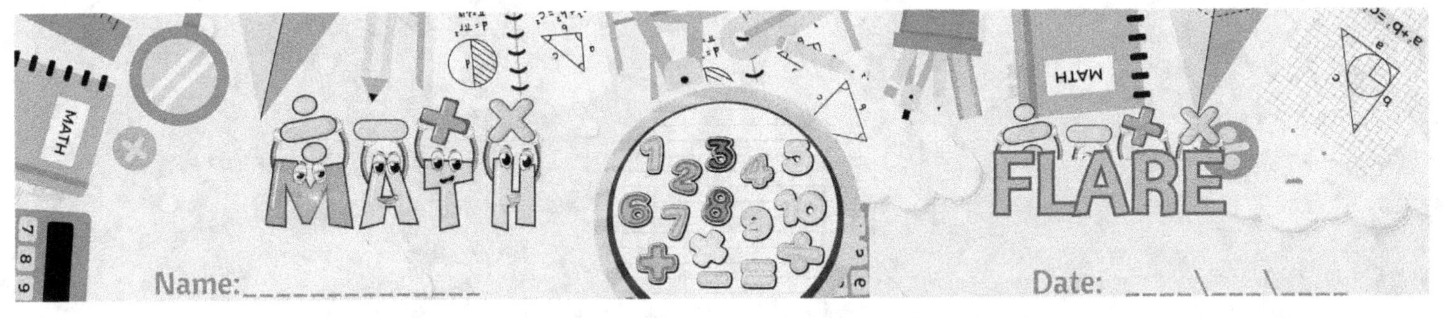

41. 731.84 + 388.69	42. 617.25 + 526.98	43. 620.20 + 240.48	44. 337.39 + 365.58
45. 648.24 + 526.44	46. 546.12 + 648.76	47. 408.22 + 819.10	48. 975.97 + 906.96
49. 599.92 + 279.53	50. 267.25 + 712.41	51. 236.13 + 653.81	52. 925.21 + 190.30
53. 882.29 + 172.51	54. 297.90 + 213.79	55. 185.55 + 300.00	56. 932.64 + 863.90
57. 417.15 + 605.67	58. 109.19 + 214.40	59. 918.68 + 308.52	60. 429.62 + 740.64

61. 623.63 + 528.31	62. 198.28 + 579.86	63. 617.07 + 129.23	64. 763.47 + 298.29
65. 670.44 + 142.62	66. 921.02 + 270.15	67. 191.30 + 787.25	68. 892.44 + 178.03
69. 463.47 + 526.95	70. 644.68 + 547.68	71. 942.57 + 223.59	72. 280.03 + 448.24
73. 593.79 + 682.21	74. 331.61 + 802.54	75. 809.91 + 861.57	76. 988.27 + 391.40
77. 849.89 + 526.61	78. 188.78 + 707.81	79. 555.53 + 445.35	80. 573.21 + 853.06

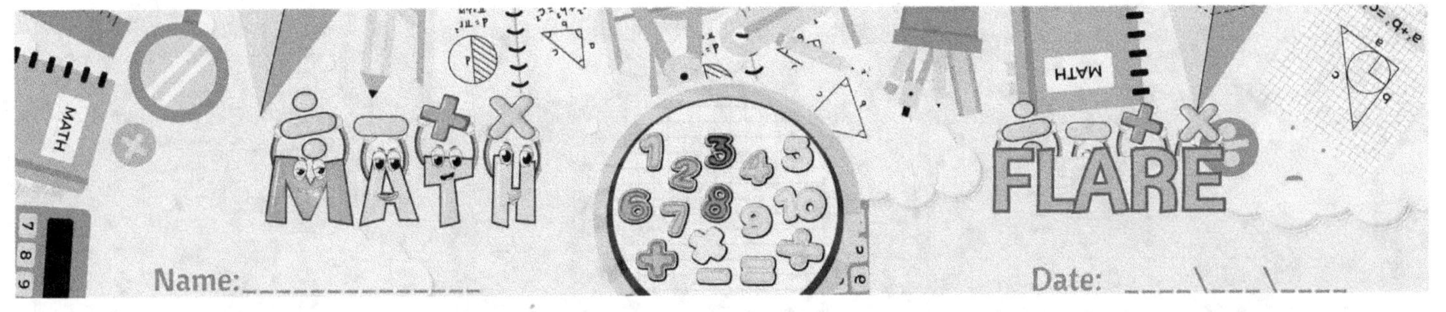

81. 409.03
   + 999.60
   ____

82. 543.34
   + 142.93
   ____

83. 378.98
   + 762.49
   ____

84. 772.60
   + 629.89
   ____

85. 713.22
   + 931.15
   ____

86. 750.91
   + 491.73
   ____

87. 663.83
   + 881.93
   ____

88. 798.06
   + 500.03
   ____

89. 348.28
   + 750.03
   ____

90. 986.06
   + 934.85
   ____

91. 797.61
   + 960.92
   ____

92. 488.37
   + 808.86
   ____

93. 154.34
   + 629.62
   ____

94. 420.24
   + 664.68
   ____

95. 698.47
   + 284.63
   ____

96. 622.49
   + 118.13
   ____

97. 953.73
   + 791.61
   ____

98. 238.65
   + 942.96
   ____

99. 680.24
   + 237.10
   ____

100. 169.26
   + 831.29
   ____

Subtracting Decimals

Find the difference.

101. 692.26 − 454.33	102. 802.28 − 776.60	103. 909.50 − 717.71	104. 572.61 − 499.09
105. 719.27 − 371.94	106. 538.79 − 389.52	107. 633.95 − 365.58	108. 962.06 − 815.91
109. 862.35 − 209.07	110. 780.91 − 226.77	111. 899.40 − 719.60	112. 738.65 − 193.24
113. 964.49 − 344.94	114. 788.25 − 366.62	115. 693.65 − 576.98	116. 353.69 − 161.13
117. 916.41 − 563.29	118. 712.61 − 245.83	119. 915.54 − 512.75	120. 468.05 − 193.60

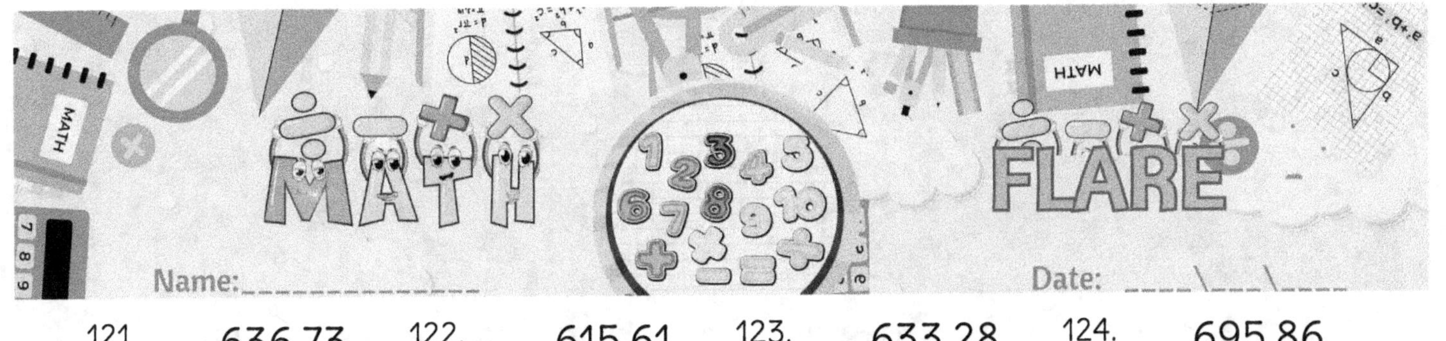

121. 636.73 − 520.84	122. 615.61 − 359.82	123. 633.28 − 356.84	124. 695.86 − 156.97
125. 899.48 − 568.26	126. 473.10 − 106.70	127. 935.72 − 171.00	128. 658.77 − 116.21
129. 729.88 − 272.81	130. 982.13 − 332.10	131. 947.67 − 167.64	132. 752.82 − 743.37
133. 816.88 − 185.67	134. 936.60 − 567.12	135. 294.11 − 217.89	136. 894.71 − 108.00
137. 880.25 − 708.05	138. 631.66 − 259.54	139. 481.97 − 159.38	140. 542.27 − 523.05

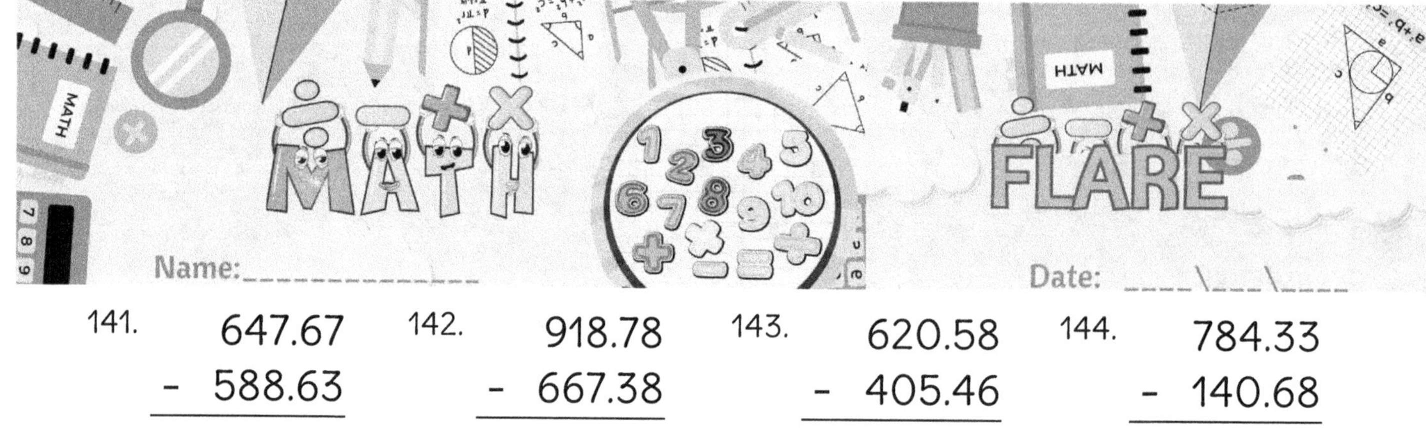

141.	647.67 - 588.63	142.	918.78 - 667.38	143.	620.58 - 405.46	144.	784.33 - 140.68
145.	418.17 - 160.68	146.	853.55 - 258.06	147.	676.78 - 540.88	148.	717.24 - 199.86
149.	451.84 - 339.62	150.	768.30 - 693.44	151.	537.99 - 447.97	152.	648.32 - 626.72
153.	989.55 - 473.60	154.	960.09 - 944.64	155.	859.58 - 796.84	156.	693.12 - 505.58
157.	609.73 - 150.07	158.	943.57 - 723.75	159.	354.17 - 264.72	160.	963.77 - 519.25

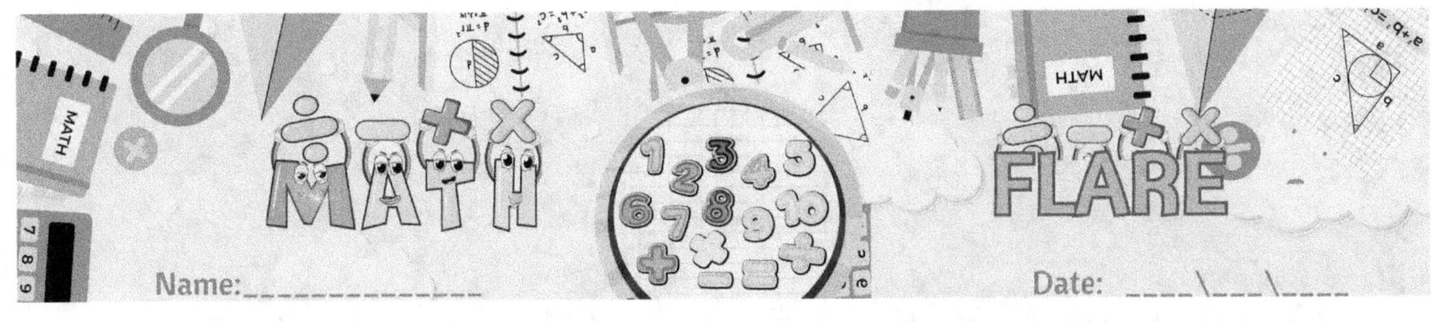

161. 722.24 − 212.73	162. 489.68 − 450.51	163. 411.17 − 316.34	164. 712.64 − 540.60
165. 767.13 − 549.05	166. 959.98 − 820.52	167. 863.86 − 532.68	168. 997.50 − 718.36
169. 707.20 − 540.84	170. 658.71 − 268.12	171. 915.39 − 866.05	172. 473.41 − 100.91
173. 738.88 − 727.23	174. 427.10 − 419.22	175. 829.70 − 632.93	176. 657.62 − 544.52
177. 793.79 − 370.28	178. 707.25 − 374.68	179. 712.31 − 292.48	180. 374.15 − 109.69

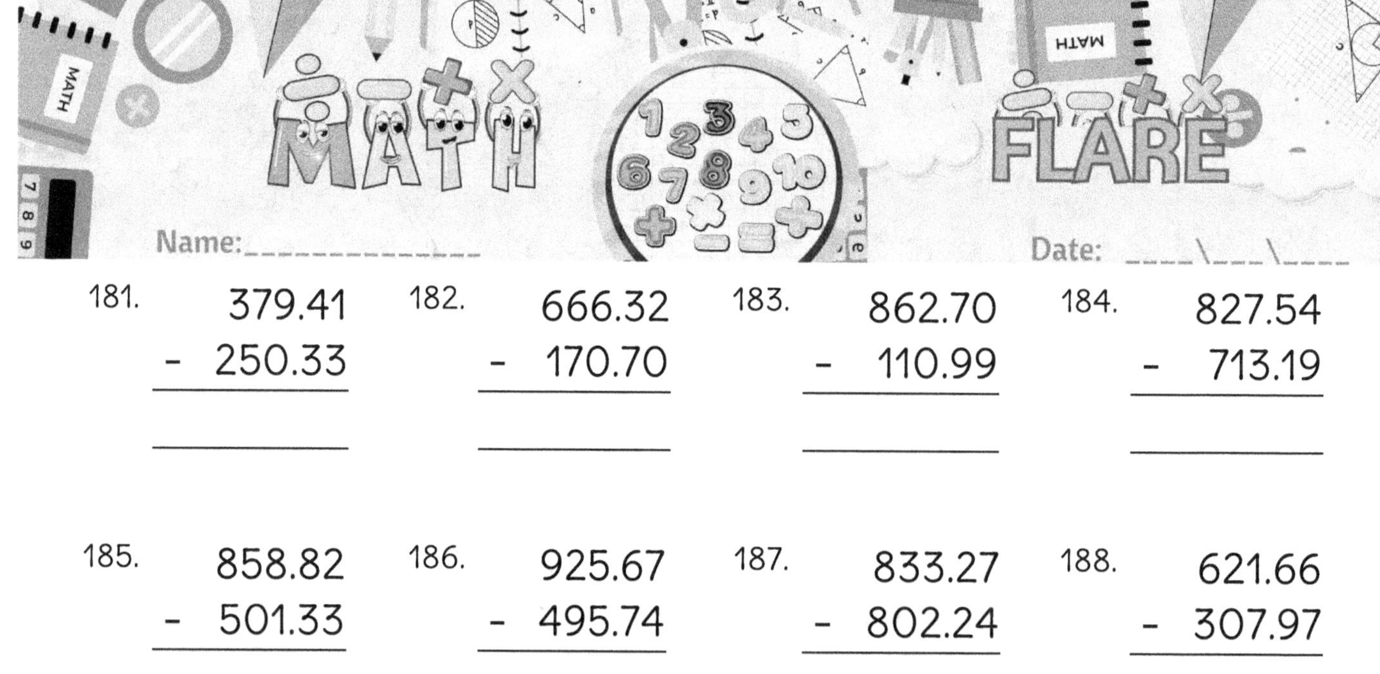

181. 379.41 − 250.33	182. 666.32 − 170.70	183. 862.70 − 110.99	184. 827.54 − 713.19
185. 858.82 − 501.33	186. 925.67 − 495.74	187. 833.27 − 802.24	188. 621.66 − 307.97
189. 728.60 − 274.55	190. 826.29 − 495.55	191. 300.67 − 240.68	192. 513.54 − 397.80
193. 898.15 − 872.81	194. 914.79 − 834.72	195. 337.42 − 160.45	196. 394.10 − 268.97
197. 974.84 − 848.44	198. 982.81 − 176.35	199. 984.58 − 684.27	200. 533.73 − 463.82

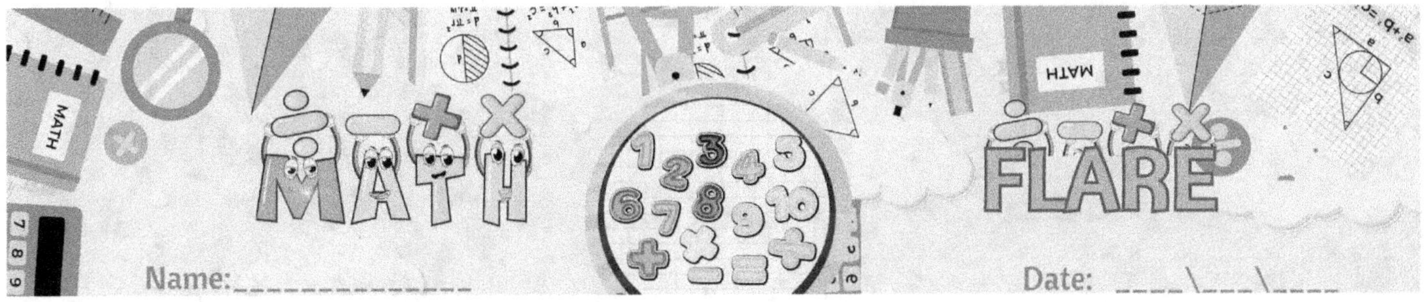

Fraction Identification

Identify fractions of each set of boxes.

201.  = ___________________________

202. = ___________________________

203. = ___________________________

204. = ___________________________

205. = ___________________________

206. = ___________________________

207. = ___________________________

208. =

____

209. =

____

210. =

____

211. =

____

212. =

____

213. =

____

214. =

____

215. =

____

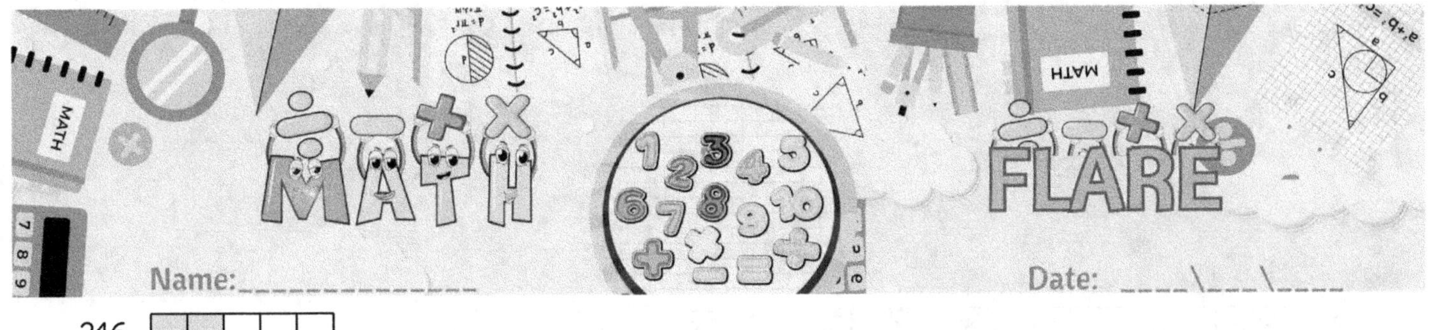

216.  =

____

217. =

____

218. =

____

219. =

____

220. 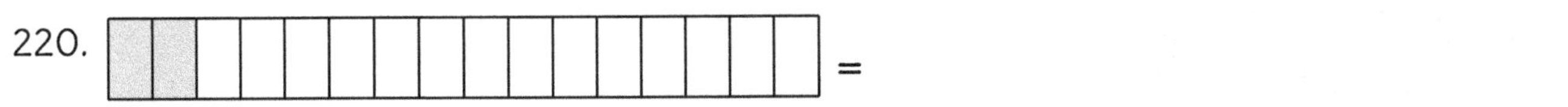 =

____

221. 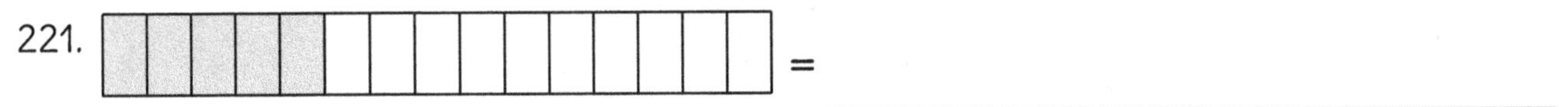 =

____

222. =

____

223. =

____

224. = ___________________

225. = ___________________

226. = ___________________

227. = ___________________

228. = ___________________

229. = ___________________

230. = ___________________

231. = ___________________

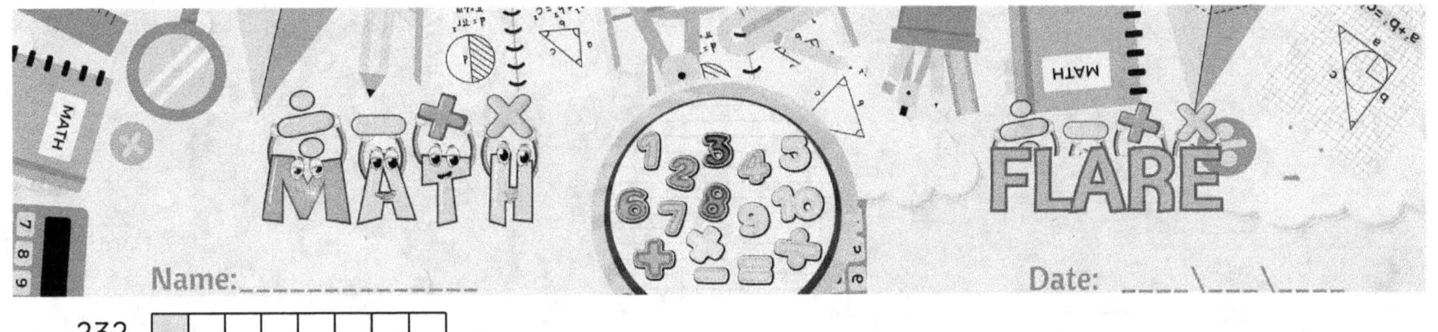

232. = __________________________

233. = __________________________

234. = __________________________

235. = __________________________

236. = __________________________

237. = __________________________

238. = __________________________

239. = __________________________

240. =

241. =

242. =

243. =

244. =

245. =

246. =

247. =

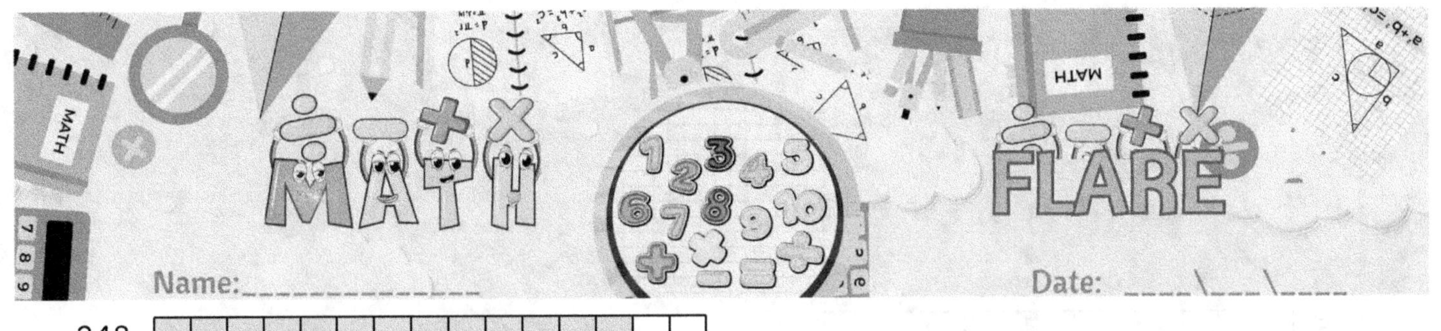

248. =

____

249. =

____

250. =

____

251. =

____

252. =

____

253. =

____

254. =

____

255. =

____

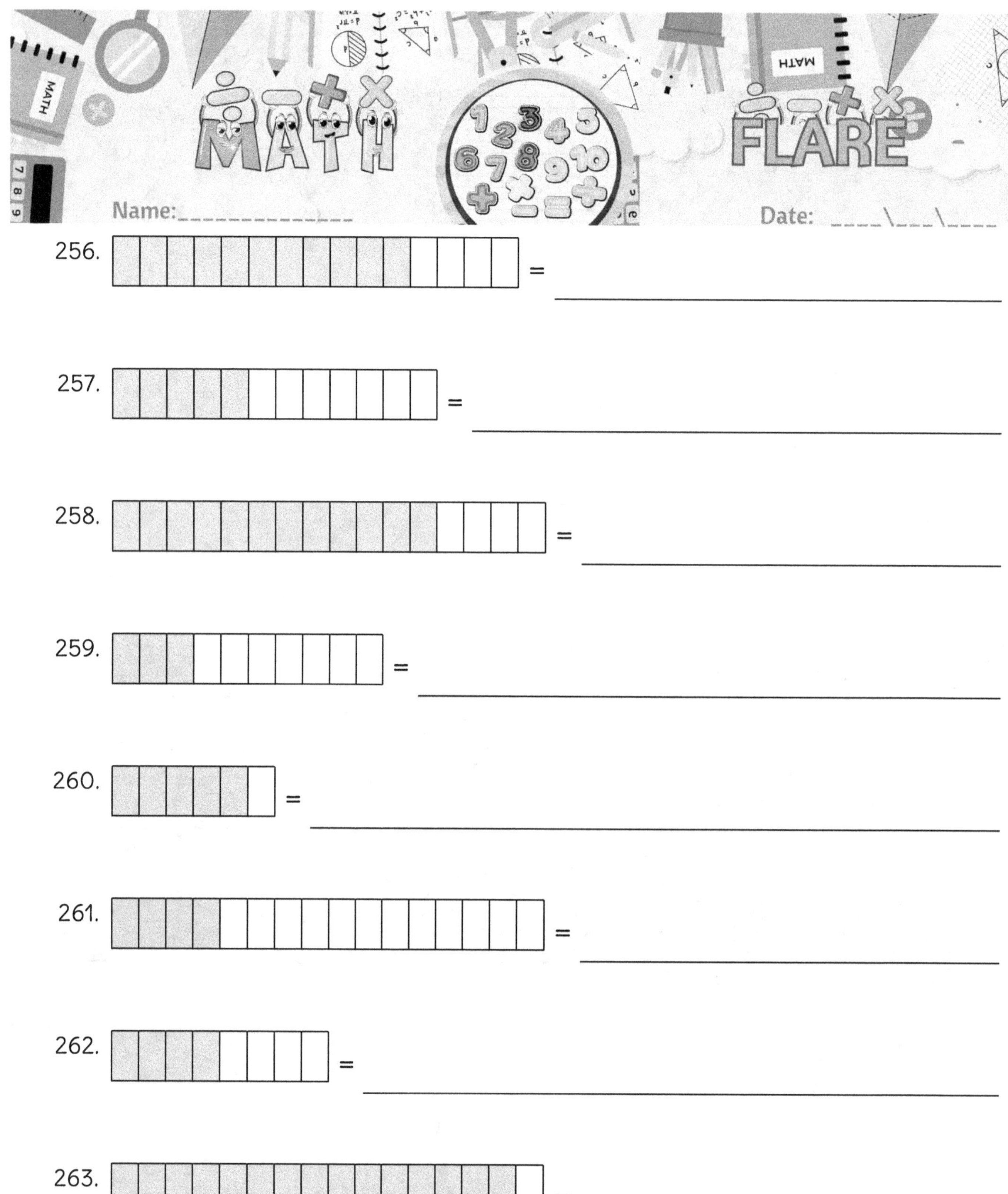

256. = _______________________

257. = _______________________

258. = _______________________

259. = _______________________

260. = _______________________

261. = _______________________

262. = _______________________

263. = _______________________

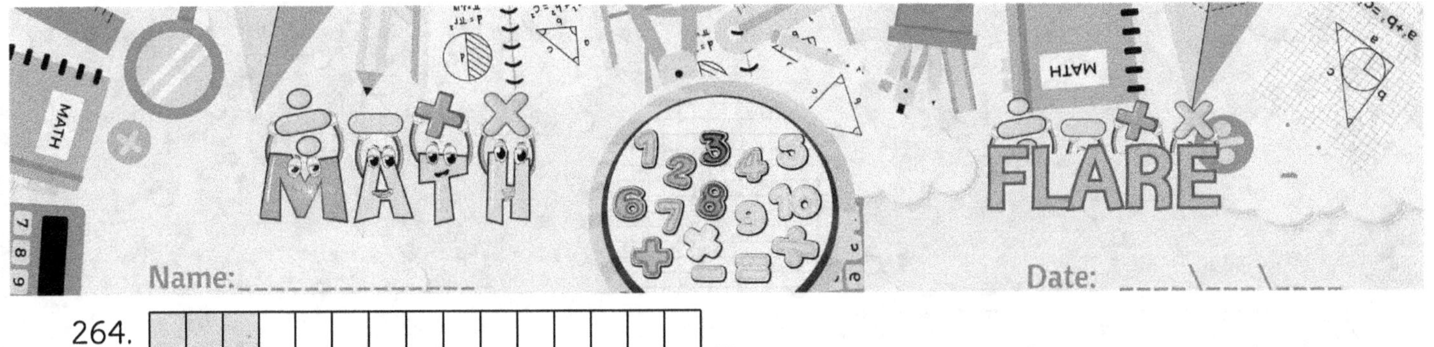

264. 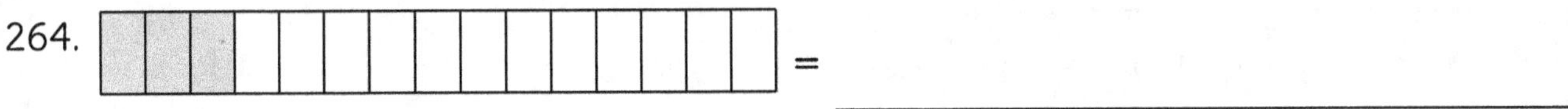 = _______________

265. 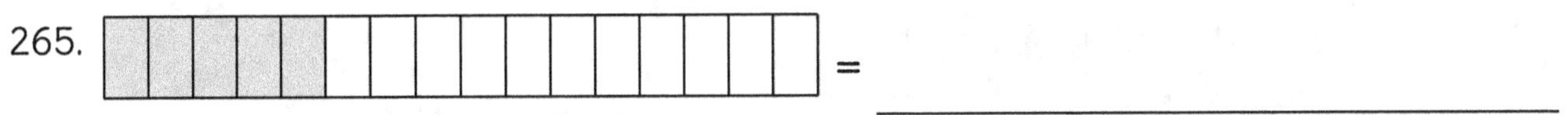 = _______________

266. = _______________

267. = _______________

268. 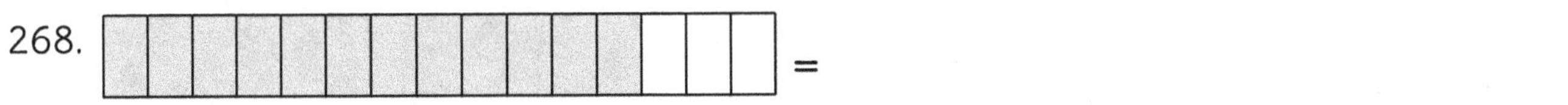 = _______________

269. = _______________

270. 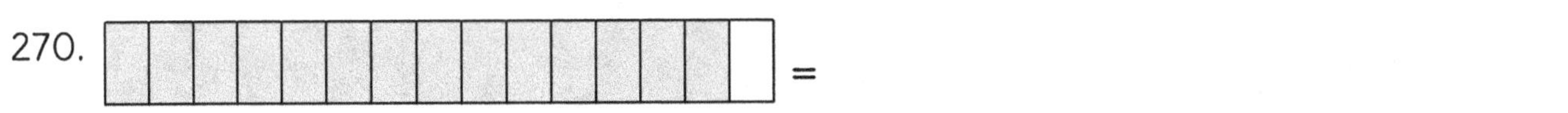 = _______________

271. = _______________

272. = __________

273. = __________

274. = __________

275. = __________

276. = __________

277. = __________

278. = __________

279. = __________

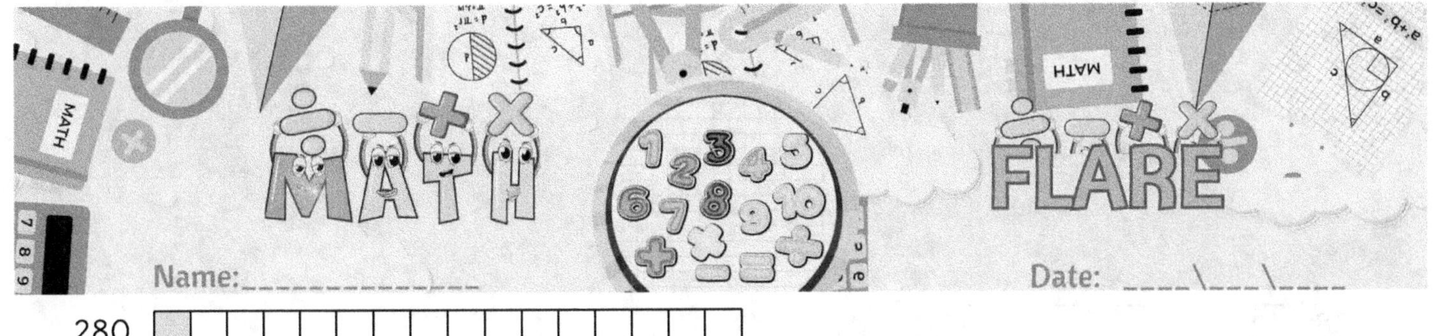

280. 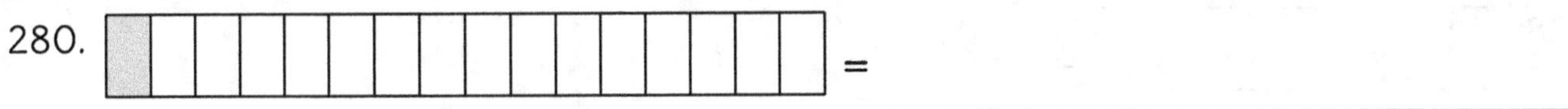 = ____________________

281. 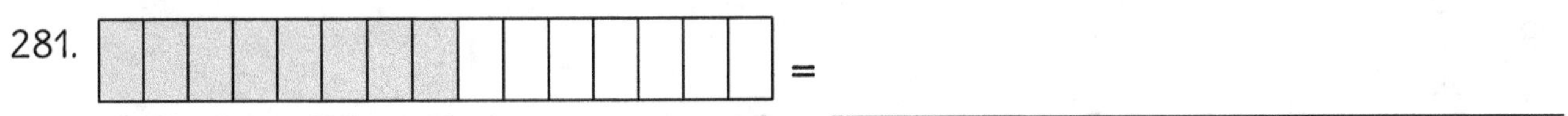 = ____________________

282. 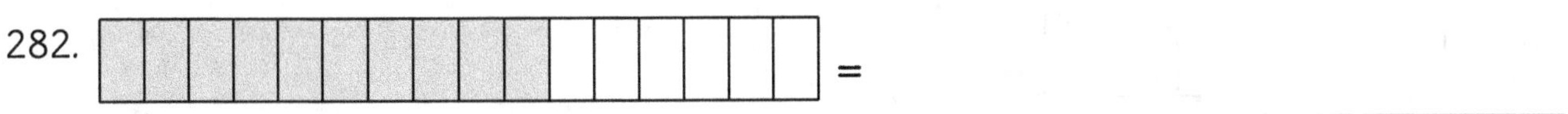 = ____________________

283. 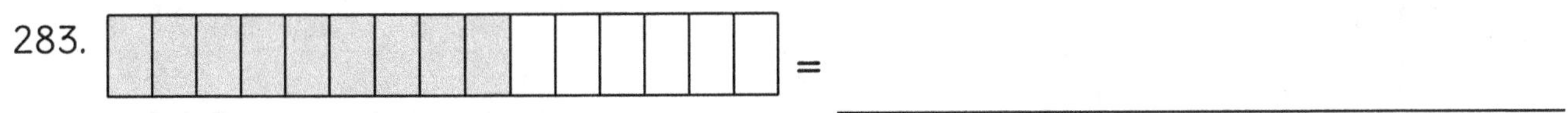 = ____________________

284. 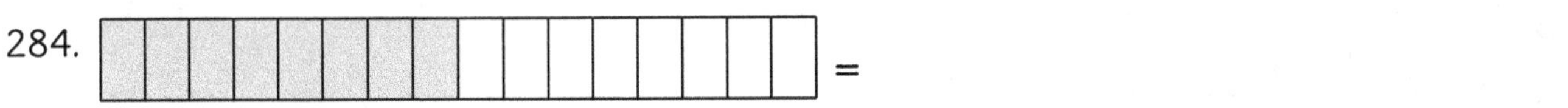 = ____________________

285. = ____________________

286. = ____________________

287. = ____________________

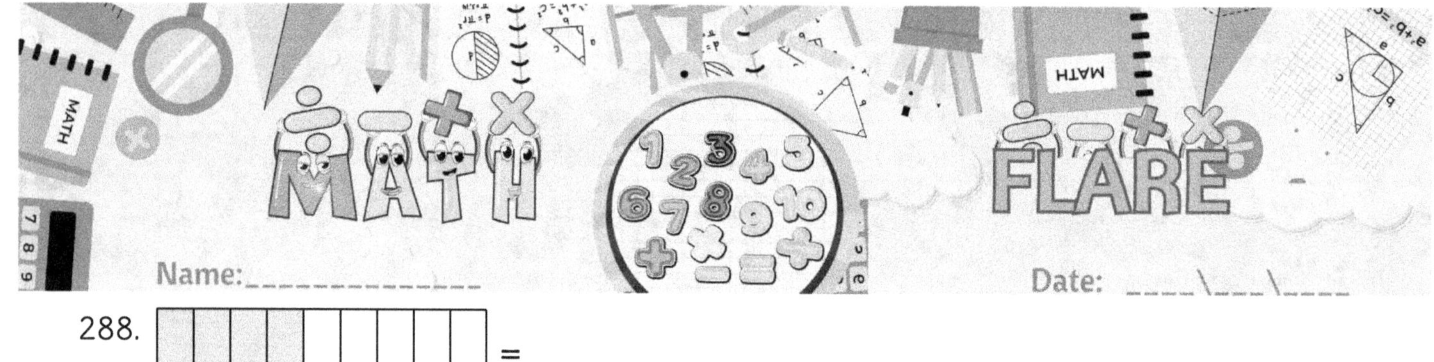

Name:_________________   Date: _______________

288. = _______________________________

289. = _______________________________

290. = _______________________________

291. = _______________________________

292. = _______________________________

293. = _______________________________

294. = _______________________________

295. = _______________________________

Compare the Fractions

Compare the fractions. Put the signs < , >, or =

296. $\dfrac{9}{60}$ ___ $\dfrac{165}{60}$

297. $\dfrac{90}{102}$ ___ $\dfrac{79}{102}$

298. $\dfrac{16}{21}$ ___ $\dfrac{19}{21}$

299. $\dfrac{4}{8}$ ___ $\dfrac{13}{8}$

300. $\dfrac{32}{17}$ ___ $\dfrac{1}{17}$

301. $\dfrac{2}{4}$ ___ $\dfrac{3}{4}$

302. $\dfrac{5}{23}$ ___ $\dfrac{6}{23}$

303. $\dfrac{35}{22}$ ___ $\dfrac{18}{22}$

304. $\dfrac{69}{72}$ ___ $\dfrac{50}{72}$

305. $\dfrac{20}{28}$ ___ $\dfrac{2}{28}$

306. $\dfrac{51}{57}$ ___ $\dfrac{8}{57}$

307. $\dfrac{33}{30}$ ___ $\dfrac{10}{30}$

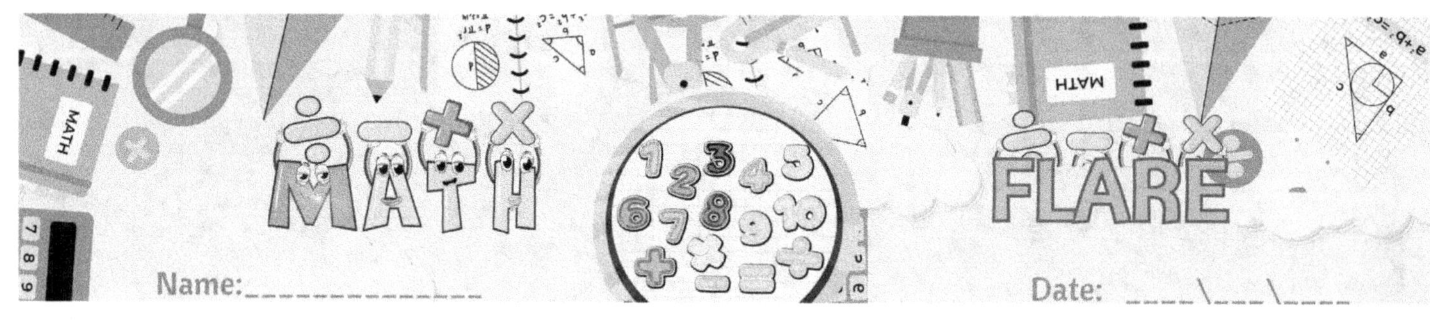

308. $\dfrac{21}{15}$ ___ $\dfrac{3}{15}$

309. $\dfrac{3}{5}$ ___ $\dfrac{2}{5}$

310. $\dfrac{13}{12}$ ___ $\dfrac{29}{12}$

311. $\dfrac{60}{65}$ ___ $\dfrac{32}{65}$

312. $\dfrac{67}{25}$ ___ $\dfrac{55}{25}$

313. $\dfrac{10}{28}$ ___ $\dfrac{9}{28}$

314. $\dfrac{60}{120}$ ___ $\dfrac{36}{120}$

315. $\dfrac{3}{9}$ ___ $\dfrac{5}{9}$

316. $\dfrac{3}{33}$ ___ $\dfrac{74}{33}$

317. $\dfrac{5}{10}$ ___ $\dfrac{24}{10}$

318. $\dfrac{6}{18}$ ___ $\dfrac{10}{18}$

319. $\dfrac{96}{126}$ ___ $\dfrac{166}{126}$

320. $\dfrac{18}{10}$ ___ $\dfrac{4}{10}$

321. $\dfrac{1}{16}$ ___ $\dfrac{18}{16}$

322. $\dfrac{5}{3}$ ___ $\dfrac{1}{3}$

323. $\dfrac{30}{36}$ ___ $\dfrac{85}{36}$

324. $\dfrac{1}{8}$ ___ $\dfrac{6}{8}$

325. $\dfrac{34}{22}$ ___ $\dfrac{47}{22}$

326. $\dfrac{80}{30}$ ___ $\dfrac{7}{30}$

327. $\dfrac{52}{68}$ ___ $\dfrac{42}{68}$

328. $\dfrac{2}{23}$ ___ $\dfrac{35}{23}$

329. $\dfrac{17}{14}$ ___ $\dfrac{12}{14}$

330. $\dfrac{3}{13}$ ___ $\dfrac{17}{13}$

331. $\dfrac{12}{36}$ ___ $\dfrac{3}{36}$

332. $\dfrac{41}{21}$ ___ $\dfrac{5}{21}$

333. $\dfrac{6}{7}$ ___ $\dfrac{5}{7}$

334. $\dfrac{20}{16}$ ___ $\dfrac{13}{16}$

335. $\dfrac{60}{125}$ ___ $\dfrac{51}{125}$

336. $\dfrac{60}{75}$ ___ $\dfrac{18}{75}$

337. $\dfrac{4}{6}$ ___ $\dfrac{13}{6}$

338. $\dfrac{24}{10}$ ___ $\dfrac{24}{10}$

339. $\dfrac{13}{9}$ ___ $\dfrac{13}{9}$

340. $\dfrac{11}{5}$ ___ $\dfrac{1}{5}$

341. $\dfrac{30}{48}$ ___ $\dfrac{31}{48}$

342. $\dfrac{29}{11}$ ___ $\dfrac{5}{11}$

343. $\dfrac{1}{3}$ ___ $\dfrac{8}{3}$

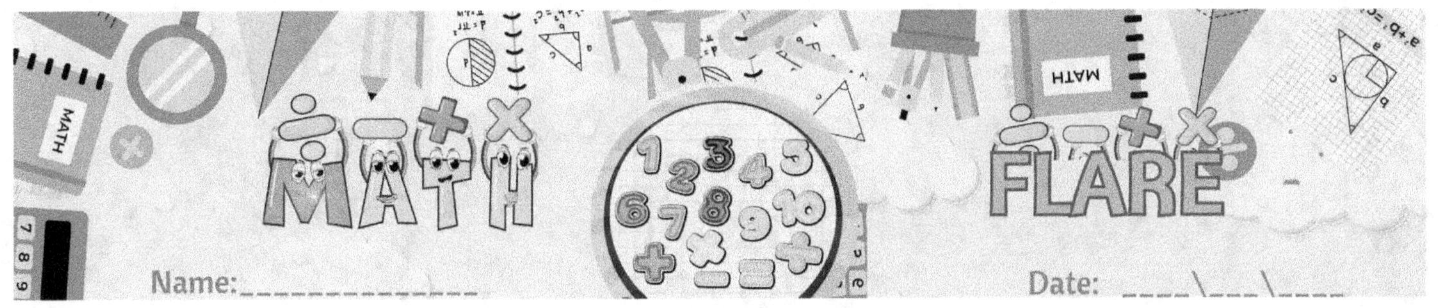

344. $\dfrac{52}{19}$ ___ $\dfrac{1}{19}$

345. $\dfrac{6}{12}$ ___ $\dfrac{7}{12}$

346. $\dfrac{3}{2}$ ___ $\dfrac{1}{2}$

347. $\dfrac{1}{4}$ ___ $\dfrac{2}{4}$

348. $\dfrac{7}{8}$ ___ $\dfrac{10}{8}$

349. $\dfrac{6}{12}$ ___ $\dfrac{8}{12}$

350. $\dfrac{7}{10}$ ___ $\dfrac{22}{10}$

351. $\dfrac{3}{22}$ ___ $\dfrac{16}{22}$

352. $\dfrac{40}{85}$ ___ $\dfrac{26}{85}$

353. $\dfrac{31}{23}$ ___ $\dfrac{9}{23}$

354. $\dfrac{1}{3}$ ___ $\dfrac{2}{3}$

355. $\dfrac{2}{15}$ ___ $\dfrac{4}{15}$

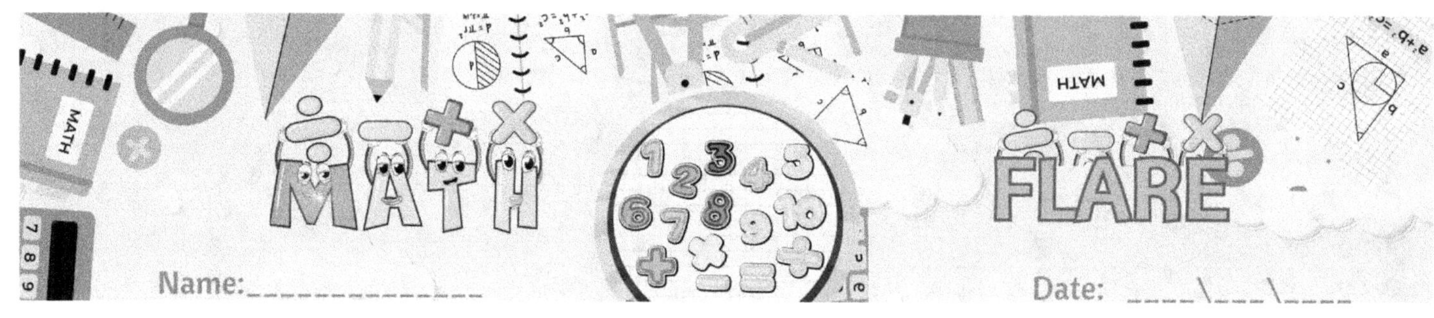

356. $\dfrac{10}{12}$ ___ $\dfrac{9}{12}$

357. $\dfrac{8}{14}$ ___ $\dfrac{12}{14}$

358. $\dfrac{59}{24}$ ___ $\dfrac{22}{24}$

359. $\dfrac{3}{9}$ ___ $\dfrac{2}{9}$

360. $\dfrac{9}{12}$ ___ $\dfrac{26}{12}$

361. $\dfrac{5}{25}$ ___ $\dfrac{38}{25}$

362. $\dfrac{90}{114}$ ___ $\dfrac{109}{114}$

363. $\dfrac{38}{16}$ ___ $\dfrac{12}{16}$

364. $\dfrac{14}{8}$ ___ $\dfrac{1}{8}$

365. $\dfrac{51}{30}$ ___ $\dfrac{11}{30}$

366. $\dfrac{19}{11}$ ___ $\dfrac{5}{11}$

367. $\dfrac{4}{20}$ ___ $\dfrac{5}{20}$

368. $\dfrac{12}{13}$ ___ $\dfrac{6}{13}$

369. $\dfrac{3}{6}$ ___ $\dfrac{10}{6}$

370. $\dfrac{4}{25}$ ___ $\dfrac{69}{25}$

371. $\dfrac{10}{7}$ ___ $\dfrac{10}{7}$

372. $\dfrac{15}{54}$ ___ $\dfrac{29}{54}$

373. $\dfrac{56}{21}$ ___ $\dfrac{49}{21}$

374. $\dfrac{3}{12}$ ___ $\dfrac{11}{12}$

375. $\dfrac{53}{25}$ ___ $\dfrac{18}{25}$

376. $\dfrac{10}{18}$ ___ $\dfrac{6}{18}$

377. $\dfrac{26}{9}$ ___ $\dfrac{8}{9}$

378. $\dfrac{35}{75}$ ___ $\dfrac{219}{75}$

379. $\dfrac{31}{23}$ ___ $\dfrac{54}{23}$

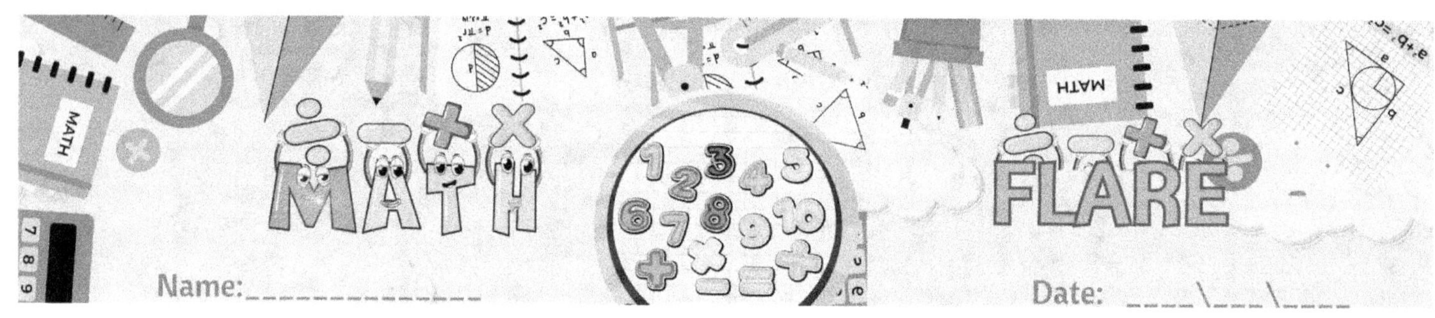

Name: _________________   Date: ____________

380. $\dfrac{16}{10}$ ___ $\dfrac{8}{10}$

381. $\dfrac{3}{14}$ ___ $\dfrac{7}{14}$

382. $\dfrac{18}{13}$ ___ $\dfrac{5}{13}$

383. $\dfrac{5}{2}$ ___ $\dfrac{1}{2}$

384. $\dfrac{6}{11}$ ___ $\dfrac{7}{11}$

385. $\dfrac{120}{144}$ ___ $\dfrac{97}{144}$

386. $\dfrac{9}{8}$ ___ $\dfrac{15}{8}$

387. $\dfrac{7}{4}$ ___ $\dfrac{5}{4}$

388. $\dfrac{84}{96}$ ___ $\dfrac{91}{96}$

389. $\dfrac{52}{68}$ ___ $\dfrac{159}{68}$

390. $\dfrac{24}{20}$ ___ $\dfrac{15}{20}$

391. $\dfrac{36}{114}$ ___ $\dfrac{332}{114}$

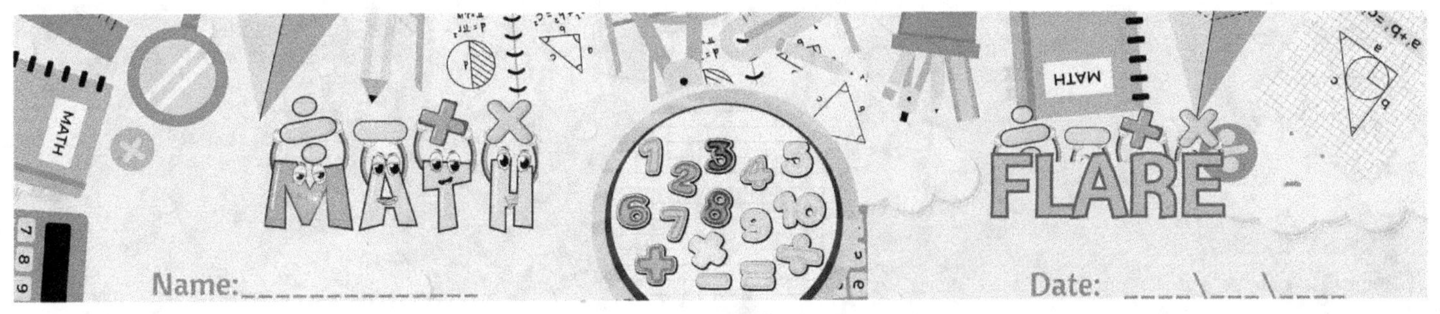

392. $\dfrac{17}{7}$ ___ $\dfrac{11}{7}$

393. $\dfrac{11}{22}$ ___ $\dfrac{10}{22}$

394. $\dfrac{9}{6}$ ___ $\dfrac{14}{6}$

395. $\dfrac{54}{30}$ ___ $\dfrac{58}{30}$

396. $\dfrac{7}{3}$ ___ $\dfrac{1}{3}$

397. $\dfrac{9}{21}$ ___ $\dfrac{50}{21}$

398. $\dfrac{2}{5}$ ___ $\dfrac{8}{5}$

399. $\dfrac{42}{60}$ ___ $\dfrac{41}{60}$

400. $\dfrac{25}{13}$ ___ $\dfrac{31}{13}$

401. $\dfrac{23}{9}$ ___ $\dfrac{7}{9}$

402. $\dfrac{1}{23}$ ___ $\dfrac{21}{23}$

403. $\dfrac{34}{16}$ ___ $\dfrac{9}{16}$

Equivalent Fractions

404. $\dfrac{7}{} = \dfrac{14}{20}$

405. $\dfrac{5}{} = \dfrac{50}{80}$

406. $\dfrac{}{9} = \dfrac{63}{81}$

407. $\dfrac{5}{7} = \dfrac{50}{}$

408. $\dfrac{11}{20} = \dfrac{110}{}$

409. $\dfrac{6}{18} = \dfrac{48}{}$

410. $\dfrac{5}{6} = \dfrac{}{12}$

411. $\dfrac{3}{} = \dfrac{9}{30}$

412. $\dfrac{}{14} = \dfrac{25}{70}$

413. $\dfrac{9}{} = \dfrac{63}{77}$

414. $\dfrac{}{15} = \dfrac{8}{120}$

415. $\dfrac{3}{} = \dfrac{15}{40}$

416. $\dfrac{8}{} = \dfrac{56}{91}$

417. $\dfrac{13}{} = \dfrac{39}{48}$

418. $\dfrac{}{2} = \dfrac{2}{4}$

419. $\dfrac{}{4} = \dfrac{18}{36}$

420. $\dfrac{3}{5} = \dfrac{}{30}$

421. $\dfrac{}{19} = \dfrac{78}{114}$

422. $\dfrac{}{12} = \dfrac{8}{24}$

423. $\dfrac{2}{} = \dfrac{6}{9}$

424. $\dfrac{7}{17} = \dfrac{}{102}$

425. $\dfrac{11}{14} = \dfrac{}{126}$

Name:_______________ Date: _____________

426. $\dfrac{10}{20} = \dfrac{}{200}$

427. $\dfrac{}{12} = \dfrac{14}{84}$

428. $\dfrac{7}{8} = \dfrac{35}{}$

429. $\dfrac{2}{4} = \dfrac{14}{}$

430. $\dfrac{1}{11} = \dfrac{}{33}$

431. $\dfrac{14}{} = \dfrac{98}{105}$

432. $\dfrac{2}{} = \dfrac{10}{25}$

433. $\dfrac{8}{9} = \dfrac{80}{}$

434. $\dfrac{2}{16} = \dfrac{12}{}$

435. $\dfrac{}{10} = \dfrac{10}{100}$

436. $\dfrac{17}{} = \dfrac{136}{152}$

437. $\dfrac{2}{3} = \dfrac{12}{}$

438. $\dfrac{13}{17} = \dfrac{}{51}$

439. $\dfrac{4}{} = \dfrac{12}{18}$

440. $\dfrac{}{13} = \dfrac{64}{104}$

441. $\dfrac{3}{} = \dfrac{18}{108}$

442. $\dfrac{1}{7} = \dfrac{}{56}$

443. $\dfrac{5}{7} = \dfrac{35}{}$

444. $\dfrac{8}{} = \dfrac{32}{48}$

445. $\dfrac{5}{} = \dfrac{30}{96}$

446. $\dfrac{2}{19} = \dfrac{}{171}$

447. $\dfrac{}{4} = \dfrac{7}{28}$

448. $\dfrac{}{8} = \dfrac{2}{16}$

449. $\dfrac{}{5} = \dfrac{6}{15}$

450. $\dfrac{9}{14} = \dfrac{}{112}$

451. $\dfrac{1}{3} = \dfrac{9}{}$

452. $\dfrac{}{10} = \dfrac{12}{30}$

453. $\dfrac{5}{15} = \dfrac{}{60}$

454. $\dfrac{5}{} = \dfrac{25}{85}$

455. $\dfrac{}{18} = \dfrac{28}{36}$

456. $\dfrac{1}{} = \dfrac{5}{45}$

457. $\dfrac{2}{} = \dfrac{18}{117}$

458. $\dfrac{}{20} = \dfrac{54}{60}$

459. $\dfrac{1}{11} = \dfrac{2}{}$

460. $\dfrac{4}{6} = \dfrac{16}{}$

461. $\dfrac{}{2} = \dfrac{6}{12}$

Fractions Addition: Common Denominator

Find the sum.

462. $\dfrac{1}{2} + \dfrac{1}{2} =$ ___________________

463. $\dfrac{1}{7} + \dfrac{1}{7} =$ ___________________

464. $\dfrac{1}{8} + \dfrac{1}{8} =$ ___________________

465. $\dfrac{1}{6} + \dfrac{4}{6} =$ ___________________

466. $\dfrac{5}{9} + \dfrac{1}{9} =$ ___________________

467. $\dfrac{2}{12} + \dfrac{7}{12} =$ ___________________

468. $\dfrac{1}{11} + \dfrac{2}{11} =$ ___________________

469. $\dfrac{1}{3} + \dfrac{1}{3} =$ ___________________

470. $\dfrac{1}{4} + \dfrac{2}{4} =$ ___________________

471. $\dfrac{2}{10} + \dfrac{3}{10} =$ ___________________

472. $\dfrac{1}{5} + \dfrac{3}{5} =$ ___________________

473. $\dfrac{1}{5} + \dfrac{1}{5} =$ ___________________

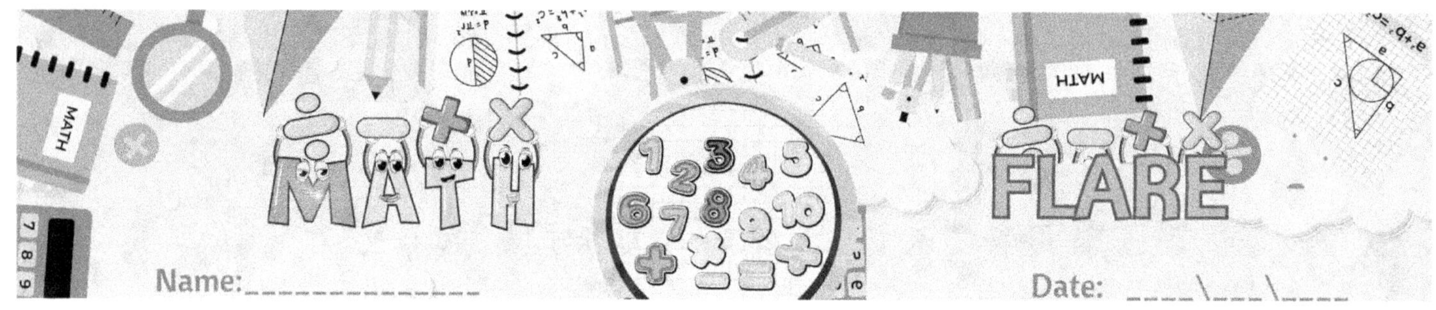

474. $\frac{2}{12} + \frac{5}{12} =$ _________________

475. $\frac{1}{9} + \frac{7}{9} =$ _________________

476. $\frac{3}{7} + \frac{2}{7} =$ _________________

477. $\frac{7}{11} + \frac{1}{11} =$ _________________

478. $\frac{3}{10} + \frac{3}{10} =$ _________________

479. $\frac{1}{4} + \frac{1}{4} =$ _________________

480. $\frac{5}{8} + \frac{2}{8} =$ _________________

481. $\frac{2}{6} + \frac{1}{6} =$ _________________

482. $\frac{1}{10} + \frac{1}{10} =$ _________________

483. $\frac{4}{9} + \frac{4}{9} =$ _________________

484. $\frac{2}{4} + \frac{1}{4} =$ _________________

485. $\frac{5}{11} + \frac{5}{11} =$ _________________

486. $\frac{4}{8} + \frac{2}{8} =$ _________________

487. $\frac{4}{12} + \frac{5}{12} =$ _________________

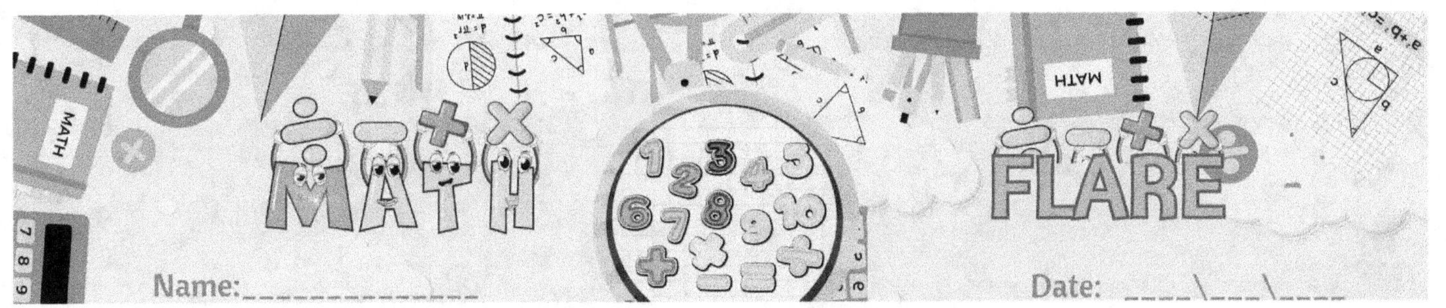

488. $\frac{1}{6} + \frac{3}{6} =$ ___________

489. $\frac{1}{7} + \frac{3}{7} =$ ___________

490. $\frac{2}{5} + \frac{2}{5} =$ ___________

491. $\frac{1}{7} + \frac{5}{7} =$ ___________

492. $\frac{1}{8} + \frac{4}{8} =$ ___________

493. $\frac{3}{12} + \frac{1}{12} =$ ___________

494. $\frac{3}{6} + \frac{2}{6} =$ ___________

495. $\frac{6}{10} + \frac{3}{10} =$ ___________

496. $\frac{2}{11} + \frac{3}{11} =$ ___________

497. $\frac{6}{9} + \frac{1}{9} =$ ___________

498. $\frac{5}{10} + \frac{4}{10} =$ ___________

499. $\frac{6}{12} + \frac{4}{12} =$ ___________

500. $\frac{1}{5} + \frac{2}{5} =$ ___________

501. $\frac{5}{11} + \frac{4}{11} =$ ___________

502. $\dfrac{3}{8} + \dfrac{2}{8} =$ _______________

503. $\dfrac{3}{12} + \dfrac{4}{12} =$ _______________

504. $\dfrac{4}{11} + \dfrac{5}{11} =$ _______________

505. $\dfrac{1}{7} + \dfrac{4}{7} =$ _______________

506. $\dfrac{2}{9} + \dfrac{4}{9} =$ _______________

507. $\dfrac{1}{9} + \dfrac{5}{9} =$ _______________

508. $\dfrac{2}{10} + \dfrac{5}{10} =$ _______________

509. $\dfrac{5}{7} + \dfrac{1}{7} =$ _______________

510. $\dfrac{3}{6} + \dfrac{1}{6} =$ _______________

511. $\dfrac{5}{11} + \dfrac{3}{11} =$ _______________

512. $\dfrac{7}{12} + \dfrac{4}{12} =$ _______________

513. $\dfrac{3}{5} + \dfrac{1}{5} =$ _______________

514. $\dfrac{1}{9} + \dfrac{1}{9} =$ _______________

515. $\dfrac{2}{8} + \dfrac{3}{8} =$ _______________

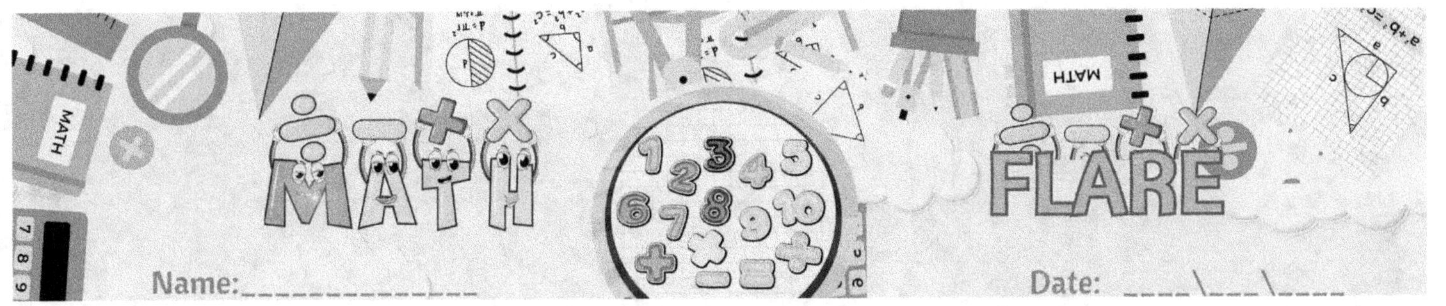

516. $\frac{6}{12} + \frac{2}{12} =$ _______________

517. $\frac{5}{10} + \frac{1}{10} =$ _______________

518. $\frac{2}{7} + \frac{1}{7} =$ _______________

519. $\frac{3}{8} + \frac{3}{8} =$ _______________

520. $\frac{3}{9} + \frac{3}{9} =$ _______________

521. $\frac{2}{5} + \frac{1}{5} =$ _______________

522. $\frac{1}{10} + \frac{2}{10} =$ _______________

523. $\frac{5}{12} + \frac{3}{12} =$ _______________

524. $\frac{2}{11} + \frac{4}{11} =$ _______________

525. $\frac{2}{6} + \frac{3}{6} =$ _______________

526. $\frac{5}{11} + \frac{2}{11} =$ _______________

527. $\frac{5}{9} + \frac{2}{9} =$ _______________

528. $\frac{5}{12} + \frac{2}{12} =$ _______________

529. $\frac{1}{7} + \frac{2}{7} =$ _______________

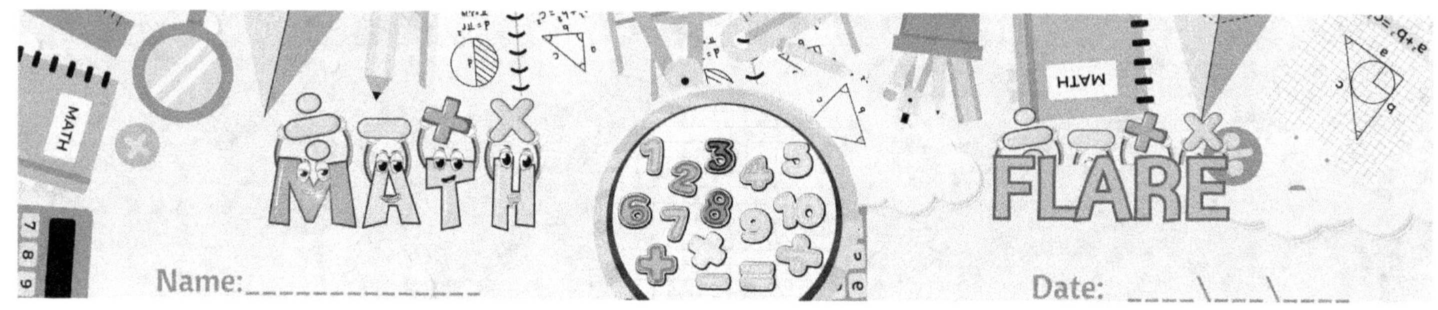

530. $\dfrac{1}{8} + \dfrac{5}{8} =$ ___________

531. $\dfrac{1}{6} + \dfrac{2}{6} =$ ___________

532. $\dfrac{2}{10} + \dfrac{4}{10} =$ ___________

533. $\dfrac{7}{12} + \dfrac{1}{12} =$ ___________

534. $\dfrac{1}{9} + \dfrac{6}{9} =$ ___________

535. $\dfrac{1}{8} + \dfrac{2}{8} =$ ___________

536. $\dfrac{8}{11} + \dfrac{1}{11} =$ ___________

537. $\dfrac{4}{10} + \dfrac{3}{10} =$ ___________

538. $\dfrac{4}{8} + \dfrac{1}{8} =$ ___________

539. $\dfrac{2}{6} + \dfrac{2}{6} =$ ___________

540. $\dfrac{1}{12} + \dfrac{9}{12} =$ ___________

541. $\dfrac{2}{9} + \dfrac{6}{9} =$ ___________

542. $\dfrac{5}{11} + \dfrac{1}{11} =$ ___________

543. $\dfrac{1}{9} + \dfrac{4}{9} =$ ___________

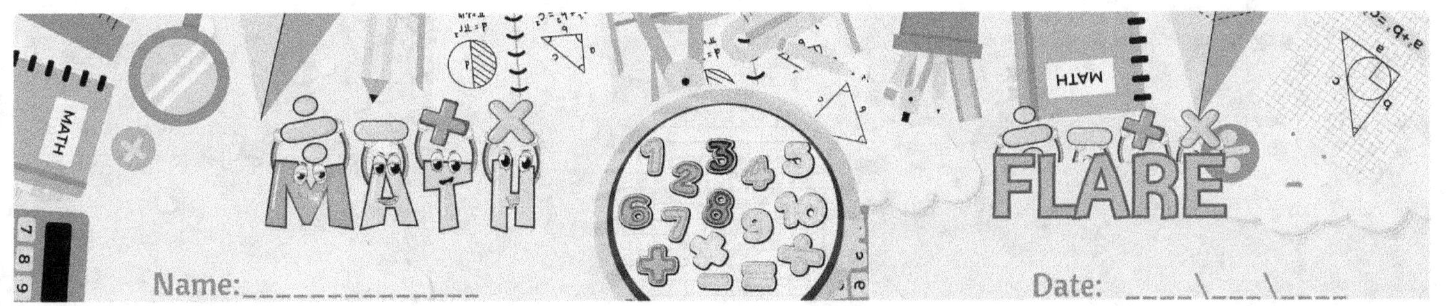

544. $\dfrac{2}{8} + \dfrac{2}{8} =$ _______________

545. $\dfrac{6}{11} + \dfrac{3}{11} =$ _______________

546. $\dfrac{7}{12} + \dfrac{3}{12} =$ _______________

547. $\dfrac{3}{10} + \dfrac{4}{10} =$ _______________

548. $\dfrac{4}{9} + \dfrac{3}{9} =$ _______________

549. $\dfrac{1}{11} + \dfrac{4}{11} =$ _______________

550. $\dfrac{3}{8} + \dfrac{1}{8} =$ _______________

551. $\dfrac{5}{12} + \dfrac{4}{12} =$ _______________

552. $\dfrac{4}{6} + \dfrac{1}{6} =$ _______________

553. $\dfrac{1}{11} + \dfrac{7}{11} =$ _______________

554. $\dfrac{2}{7} + \dfrac{3}{7} =$ _______________

555. $\dfrac{2}{9} + \dfrac{2}{9} =$ _______________

556. $\dfrac{4}{9} + \dfrac{2}{9} =$ _______________

557. $\dfrac{10}{12} + \dfrac{1}{12} =$ _______________

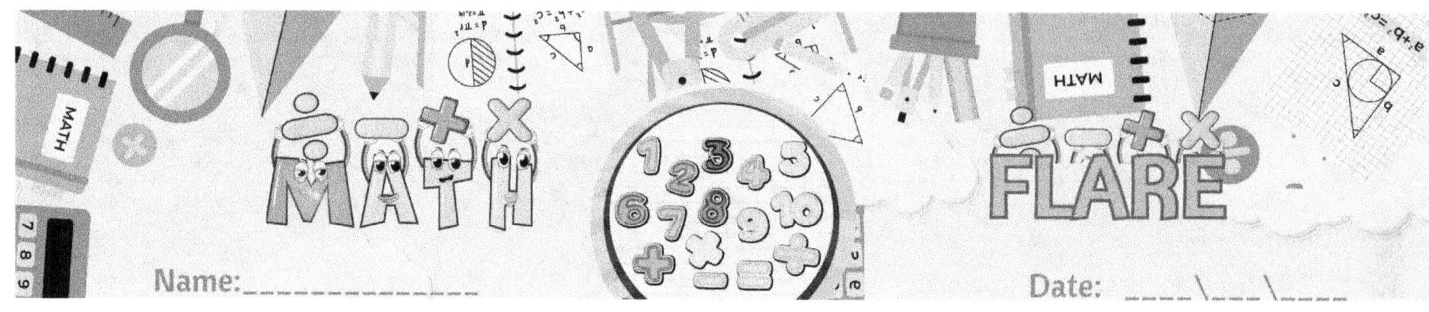

Fractions Subtraction - Common Denominator

Find the difference.

558. $\dfrac{2}{3} - \dfrac{1}{3} =$ _______________

559. $\dfrac{11}{12} - \dfrac{6}{12} =$ _______________

560. $\dfrac{8}{11} - \dfrac{3}{11} =$ _______________

561. $\dfrac{7}{9} - \dfrac{5}{9} =$ _______________

562. $\dfrac{2}{5} - \dfrac{1}{5} =$ _______________

563. $\dfrac{7}{8} - \dfrac{6}{8} =$ _______________

564. $\dfrac{5}{7} - \dfrac{4}{7} =$ _______________

565. $\dfrac{5}{6} - \dfrac{2}{6} =$ _______________

566. $\dfrac{4}{5} - \dfrac{3}{5} =$ _______________

567. $\dfrac{4}{10} - \dfrac{2}{10} =$ _______________

568. $\dfrac{3}{4} - \dfrac{1}{4} =$ _______________

569. $\dfrac{5}{12} - \dfrac{1}{12} =$ _______________

570. $\dfrac{8}{11} - \dfrac{6}{11} =$ _______________

571. $\dfrac{8}{9} - \dfrac{4}{9} =$ _______________

572. $\dfrac{3}{11} - \dfrac{2}{11} =$ _______________

573. $\dfrac{2}{4} - \dfrac{1}{4} =$ _______________

574. $\dfrac{5}{6} - \dfrac{4}{6} =$ _______________

575. $\dfrac{7}{10} - \dfrac{6}{10} =$ _______________

576. $\dfrac{6}{9} - \dfrac{4}{9} =$ _______________

577. $\dfrac{3}{5} - \dfrac{1}{5} =$ _______________

578. $\dfrac{10}{12} - \dfrac{9}{12} =$ _______________

579. $\dfrac{6}{7} - \dfrac{3}{7} =$ _______________

580. $\dfrac{6}{8} - \dfrac{2}{8} =$ _______________

581. $\dfrac{3}{5} - \dfrac{2}{5} =$ _______________

582. $\dfrac{11}{12} - \dfrac{9}{12} =$ _______________

583. $\dfrac{5}{6} - \dfrac{1}{6} =$ _______________

584. $\dfrac{6}{7} - \dfrac{4}{7} =$ _______________

585. $\dfrac{3}{10} - \dfrac{1}{10} =$ _______________

586. $\dfrac{10}{11} - \dfrac{9}{11} =$ _______________

587. $\dfrac{8}{9} - \dfrac{7}{9} =$ _______________

588. $\dfrac{4}{7} - \dfrac{1}{7} =$ _______________

589. $\dfrac{9}{10} - \dfrac{8}{10} =$ _______________

590. $\dfrac{3}{4} - \dfrac{2}{4} =$ _______________

591. $\dfrac{5}{6} - \dfrac{3}{6} =$ _______________

592. $\dfrac{6}{8} - \dfrac{4}{8} =$ _______________

593. $\dfrac{11}{12} - \dfrac{5}{12} =$ _______________

594. $\dfrac{11}{12} - \dfrac{8}{12} =$ _______________

595. $\dfrac{3}{6} - \dfrac{1}{6} =$ _______________

596. $\dfrac{8}{9} - \dfrac{3}{9} =$ _______________

597. $\dfrac{4}{7} - \dfrac{3}{7} =$ _______________

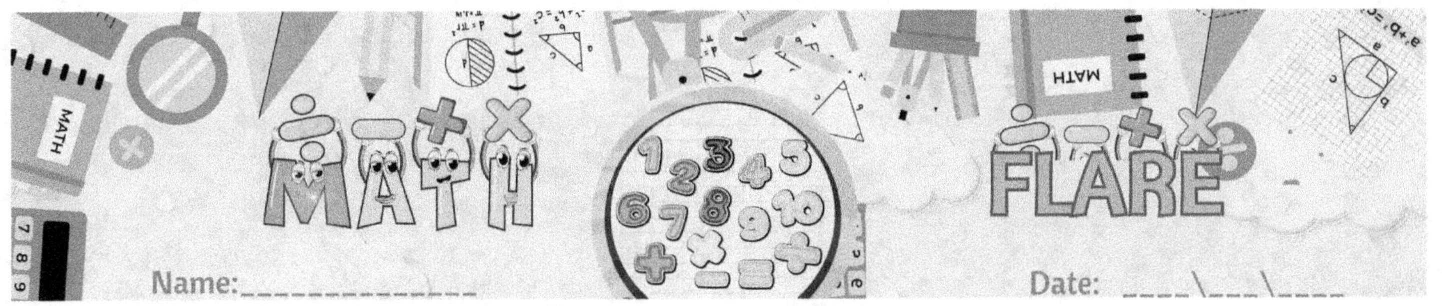

598. $\dfrac{6}{10} - \dfrac{3}{10} =$ _______________

599. $\dfrac{7}{11} - \dfrac{6}{11} =$ _______________

600. $\dfrac{7}{8} - \dfrac{4}{8} =$ _______________

601. $\dfrac{10}{11} - \dfrac{8}{11} =$ _______________

602. $\dfrac{7}{9} - \dfrac{3}{9} =$ _______________

603. $\dfrac{9}{10} - \dfrac{6}{10} =$ _______________

604. $\dfrac{4}{8} - \dfrac{2}{8} =$ _______________

605. $\dfrac{5}{8} - \dfrac{4}{8} =$ _______________

606. $\dfrac{3}{6} - \dfrac{2}{6} =$ _______________

607. $\dfrac{6}{7} - \dfrac{5}{7} =$ _______________

608. $\dfrac{8}{12} - \dfrac{4}{12} =$ _______________

609. $\dfrac{7}{10} - \dfrac{2}{10} =$ _______________

610. $\dfrac{7}{8} - \dfrac{5}{8} =$ _______________

611. $\dfrac{8}{9} - \dfrac{2}{9} =$ _______________

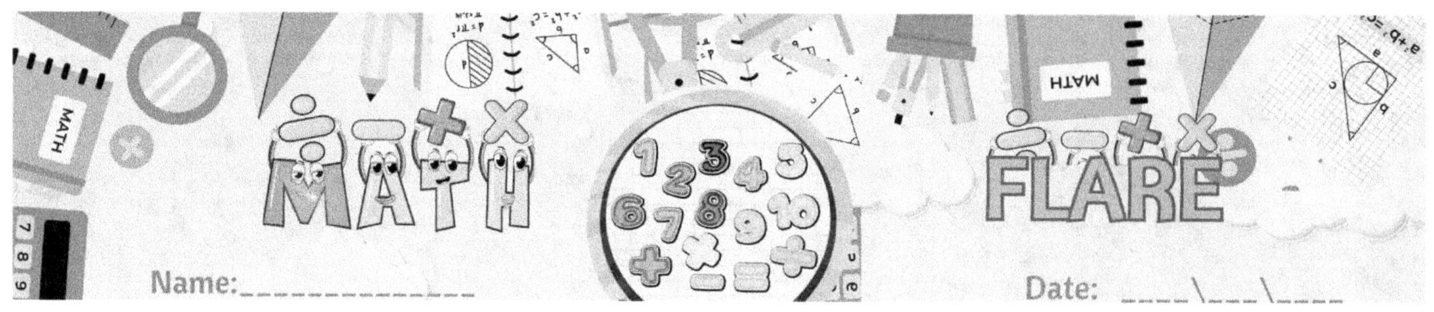

612. $\dfrac{2}{7} - \dfrac{1}{7} =$ _______________

613. $\dfrac{9}{10} - \dfrac{4}{10} =$ _______________

614. $\dfrac{4}{9} - \dfrac{1}{9} =$ _______________

615. $\dfrac{4}{7} - \dfrac{2}{7} =$ _______________

616. $\dfrac{7}{10} - \dfrac{4}{10} =$ _______________

617. $\dfrac{10}{11} - \dfrac{7}{11} =$ _______________

618. $\dfrac{9}{12} - \dfrac{2}{12} =$ _______________

619. $\dfrac{4}{5} - \dfrac{1}{5} =$ _______________

620. $\dfrac{9}{10} - \dfrac{1}{10} =$ _______________

621. $\dfrac{8}{11} - \dfrac{5}{11} =$ _______________

622. $\dfrac{7}{8} - \dfrac{3}{8} =$ _______________

623. $\dfrac{8}{12} - \dfrac{7}{12} =$ _______________

624. $\dfrac{9}{11} - \dfrac{7}{11} =$ _______________

625. $\dfrac{8}{10} - \dfrac{6}{10} =$ _______________

626. $\dfrac{6}{11} - \dfrac{3}{11} =$ _______________

627. $\dfrac{6}{7} - \dfrac{2}{7} =$ _______________

628. $\dfrac{4}{12} - \dfrac{1}{12} =$ _______________

629. $\dfrac{8}{10} - \dfrac{5}{10} =$ _______________

630. $\dfrac{8}{9} - \dfrac{1}{9} =$ _______________

631. $\dfrac{7}{8} - \dfrac{1}{8} =$ _______________

632. $\dfrac{4}{6} - \dfrac{2}{6} =$ _______________

633. $\dfrac{3}{9} - \dfrac{2}{9} =$ _______________

634. $\dfrac{9}{11} - \dfrac{5}{11} =$ _______________

635. $\dfrac{4}{12} - \dfrac{2}{12} =$ _______________

636. $\dfrac{4}{9} - \dfrac{2}{9} =$ _______________

637. $\dfrac{9}{11} - \dfrac{6}{11} =$ _______________

638. $\dfrac{5}{8} - \dfrac{1}{8} =$ _______________

639. $\dfrac{2}{6} - \dfrac{1}{6} =$ _______________

Name:________________   Date: _______________

640. $\dfrac{9}{11} - \dfrac{8}{11} =$ _________________

641. $\dfrac{2}{10} - \dfrac{1}{10} =$ _________________

642. $\dfrac{8}{12} - \dfrac{2}{12} =$ _________________

643. $\dfrac{8}{10} - \dfrac{3}{10} =$ _________________

644. $\dfrac{6}{9} - \dfrac{5}{9} =$ _________________

645. $\dfrac{5}{7} - \dfrac{1}{7} =$ _________________

646. $\dfrac{7}{12} - \dfrac{6}{12} =$ _________________

647. $\dfrac{3}{10} - \dfrac{2}{10} =$ _________________

648. $\dfrac{4}{11} - \dfrac{1}{11} =$ _________________

649. $\dfrac{8}{9} - \dfrac{6}{9} =$ _________________

650. $\dfrac{11}{12} - \dfrac{10}{12} =$ _________________

651. $\dfrac{6}{8} - \dfrac{3}{8} =$ _________________

652. $\dfrac{5}{10} - \dfrac{3}{10} =$ _________________

653. $\dfrac{4}{6} - \dfrac{1}{6} =$ _________________

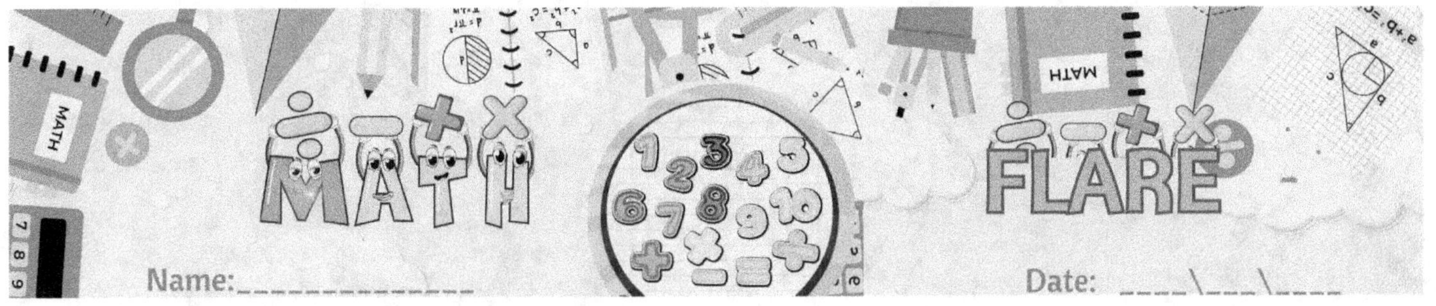

Fractions Multiplication

Find the product.

654. $\dfrac{7}{8} \times \dfrac{3}{5} =$ ________________

655. $\dfrac{3}{4} \times \dfrac{1}{2} =$ ________________

656. $\dfrac{2}{7} \times \dfrac{5}{6} =$ ________________

657. $\dfrac{1}{11} \times \dfrac{4}{7} =$ ________________

658. $\dfrac{7}{8} \times \dfrac{9}{11} =$ ________________

659. $\dfrac{2}{3} \times \dfrac{2}{3} =$ ________________

660. $\dfrac{9}{10} \times \dfrac{4}{9} =$ ________________

661. $\dfrac{5}{6} \times \dfrac{1}{2} =$ ________________

662. $\dfrac{1}{3} \times \dfrac{4}{5} =$ ________________

663. $\dfrac{8}{11} \times \dfrac{5}{6} =$ ________________

664. $\dfrac{3}{8} \times \dfrac{2}{7} =$ _______________

665. $\dfrac{5}{6} \times \dfrac{2}{3} =$ _______________

666. $\dfrac{1}{2} \times \dfrac{7}{9} =$ _______________

667. $\dfrac{2}{5} \times \dfrac{1}{2} =$ _______________

668. $\dfrac{1}{2} \times \dfrac{1}{12} =$ _______________

669. $\dfrac{2}{3} \times \dfrac{5}{8} =$ _______________

670. $\dfrac{7}{10} \times \dfrac{2}{3} =$ _______________

671. $\dfrac{2}{11} \times \dfrac{1}{5} =$ _______________

672. $\dfrac{6}{7} \times \dfrac{1}{12} =$ _______________

673. $\dfrac{6}{7} \times \dfrac{1}{2} =$ _______________

674. $\dfrac{5}{12} \times \dfrac{2}{3} =$ _______________

675. $\dfrac{3}{5} \times \dfrac{9}{11} =$ _______________

676. $\dfrac{2}{3} \times \dfrac{4}{5} =$ _______________

677. $\dfrac{1}{6} \times \dfrac{6}{11} =$ _______________

678. $\dfrac{3}{5} \times \dfrac{1}{3} =$ _______________

679. $\dfrac{1}{4} \times \dfrac{5}{7} =$ _______________

680. $\dfrac{3}{4} \times \dfrac{1}{4} =$ _______________

681. $\dfrac{5}{9} \times \dfrac{1}{2} =$ _______________

682. $\dfrac{2}{3} \times \dfrac{1}{2} =$ _______________

683. $\dfrac{2}{3} \times \dfrac{3}{4} =$ _______________

684. $\dfrac{5}{6} \times \dfrac{2}{7} =$ _______________

685. $\dfrac{6}{7} \times \dfrac{2}{5} =$ _______________

686. $\dfrac{2}{5} \times \dfrac{5}{8} =$ _______________

687. $\dfrac{1}{2} \times \dfrac{3}{11} =$ _______________

688. $\dfrac{4}{5} \times \dfrac{3}{4} =$ _______________

689. $\dfrac{2}{3} \times \dfrac{7}{9} =$ _______________

690. $\dfrac{7}{8} \times \dfrac{1}{12} =$ _______________

691. $\dfrac{2}{7} \times \dfrac{3}{4} =$ _______________

692. $\dfrac{1}{6} \times \dfrac{2}{3} =$ _______________

693. $\dfrac{7}{10} \times \dfrac{4}{11} =$ _______________

694. $\dfrac{1}{7} \times \dfrac{1}{2} =$ _______________

695. $\dfrac{1}{6} \times \dfrac{1}{2} =$ _______________

696. $\dfrac{3}{5} \times \dfrac{1}{2} =$ _______________

697. $\dfrac{5}{11} \times \dfrac{2}{3} =$ _______________

698. $\dfrac{5}{12} \times \dfrac{2}{5} =$ _______________

699. $\dfrac{4}{9} \times \dfrac{1}{3} =$ _______________

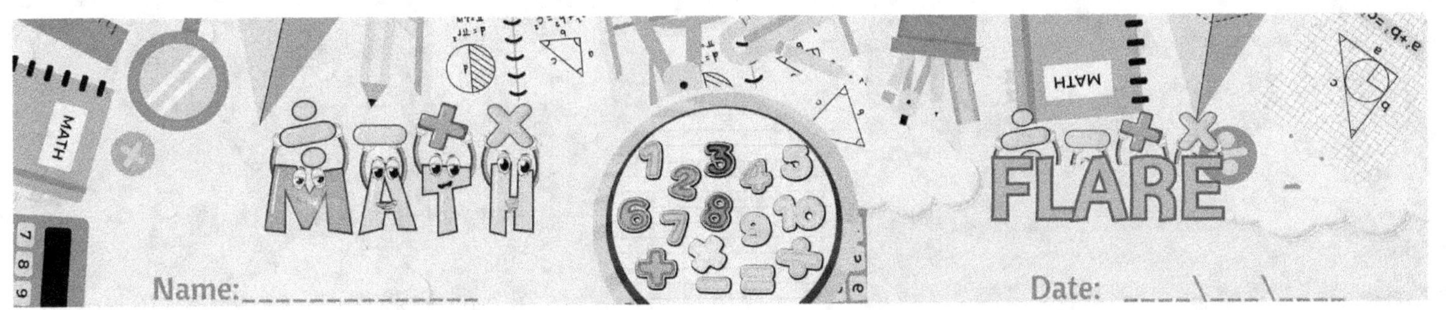

700. $\dfrac{10}{11} \times \dfrac{5}{8} =$ _______________

701. $\dfrac{7}{8} \times \dfrac{5}{11} =$ _______________

702. $\dfrac{11}{12} \times \dfrac{2}{5} =$ _______________

703. $\dfrac{3}{7} \times \dfrac{1}{6} =$ _______________

704. $\dfrac{1}{2} \times \dfrac{2}{3} =$ _______________

705. $\dfrac{1}{2} \times \dfrac{3}{4} =$ _______________

706. $\dfrac{3}{7} \times \dfrac{3}{11} =$ _______________

707. $\dfrac{9}{10} \times \dfrac{3}{4} =$ _______________

708. $\dfrac{5}{11} \times \dfrac{11}{12} =$ _______________

709. $\dfrac{1}{2} \times \dfrac{1}{2} =$ _______________

710. $\dfrac{1}{5} \times \dfrac{3}{7} =$ _______________

711. $\dfrac{7}{8} \times \dfrac{9}{10} =$ _______________

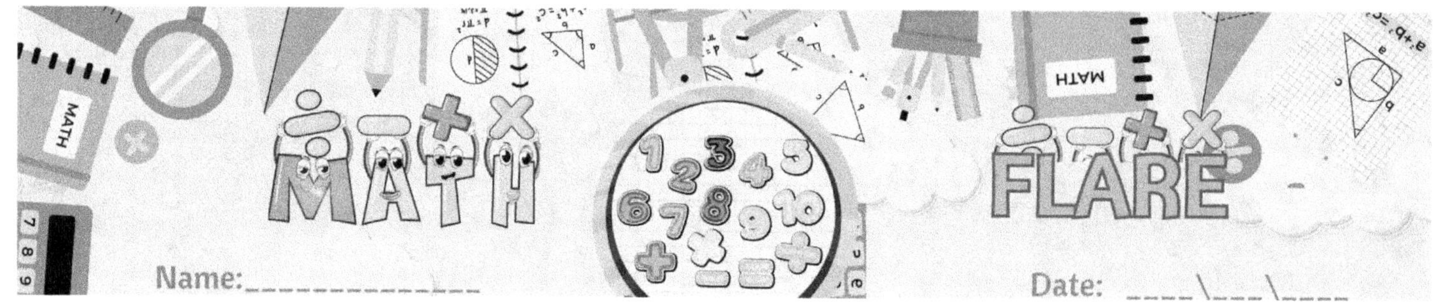

Fractions Division

Find the quotient.

712. $\dfrac{1}{12} \div \dfrac{3}{12} =$ _______________

713. $\dfrac{6}{7} \div \dfrac{4}{9} =$ _______________

714. $\dfrac{1}{12} \div \dfrac{5}{10} =$ _______________

715. $\dfrac{10}{11} \div \dfrac{1}{3} =$ _______________

716. $\dfrac{1}{2} \div \dfrac{1}{2} =$ _______________

717. $\dfrac{7}{9} \div \dfrac{8}{11} =$ _______________

718. $\dfrac{1}{3} \div \dfrac{5}{7} =$ _______________

719. $\dfrac{4}{9} \div \dfrac{3}{10} =$ _______________

720. $\dfrac{3}{4} \div \dfrac{2}{9} =$ _______________

721. $\dfrac{9}{10} \div \dfrac{1}{3} =$ _______________

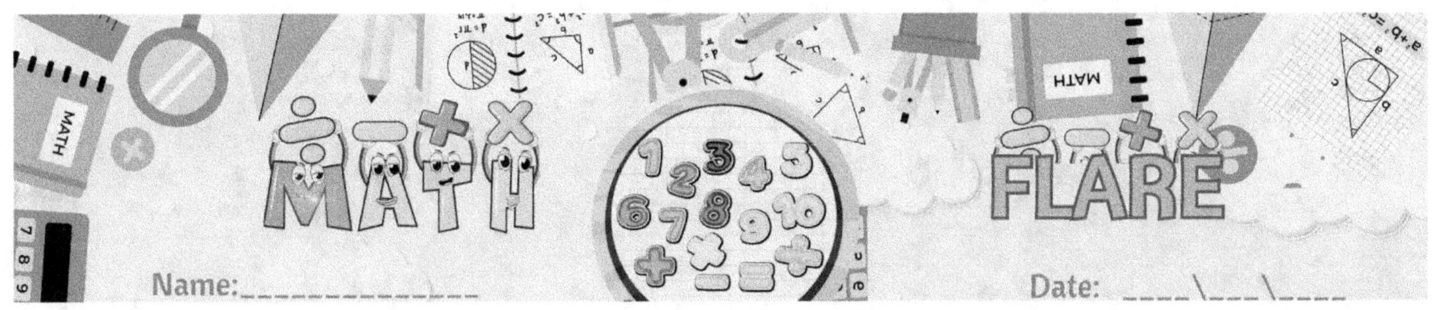

722. $\dfrac{7}{12} \div \dfrac{8}{11} =$ _______________

723. $\dfrac{4}{7} \div \dfrac{3}{5} =$ _______________

724. $\dfrac{4}{5} \div \dfrac{2}{5} =$ _______________

725. $\dfrac{3}{5} \div \dfrac{2}{4} =$ _______________

726. $\dfrac{3}{4} \div \dfrac{1}{2} =$ _______________

727. $\dfrac{1}{12} \div \dfrac{4}{7} =$ _______________

728. $\dfrac{5}{11} \div \dfrac{7}{12} =$ _______________

729. $\dfrac{2}{3} \div \dfrac{5}{9} =$ _______________

730. $\dfrac{10}{11} \div \dfrac{1}{9} =$ _______________

731. $\dfrac{3}{5} \div \dfrac{7}{8} =$ _______________

732. $\dfrac{3}{7} \div \dfrac{5}{10} =$ _______________

733. $\dfrac{2}{3} \div \dfrac{1}{5} =$ _______________

Name:________________ Date: ____________

734. $\dfrac{8}{9} \div \dfrac{1}{2} =$ _________________

735. $\dfrac{5}{6} \div \dfrac{1}{9} =$ _________________

736. $\dfrac{2}{3} \div \dfrac{4}{8} =$ _________________

737. $\dfrac{5}{9} \div \dfrac{10}{12} =$ _________________

738. $\dfrac{1}{2} \div \dfrac{7}{11} =$ _________________

739. $\dfrac{1}{12} \div \dfrac{1}{3} =$ _________________

740. $\dfrac{3}{5} \div \dfrac{1}{2} =$ _________________

741. $\dfrac{6}{11} \div \dfrac{6}{8} =$ _________________

742. $\dfrac{5}{6} \div \dfrac{3}{7} =$ _________________

743. $\dfrac{2}{5} \div \dfrac{2}{4} =$ _________________

744. $\dfrac{3}{8} \div \dfrac{2}{5} =$ _________________

745. $\dfrac{1}{12} \div \dfrac{6}{12} =$ _________________

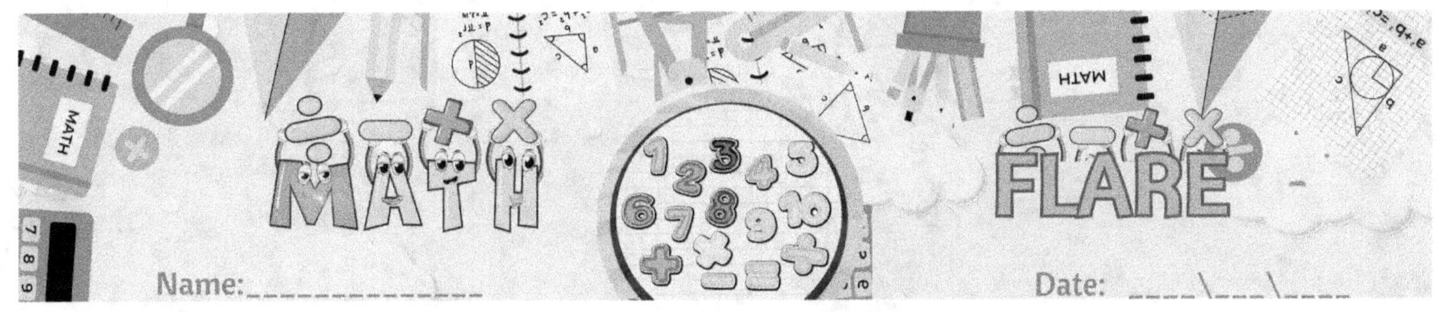

746. $\frac{7}{10} \div \frac{9}{11} =$ _______________

747. $\frac{3}{10} \div \frac{4}{6} =$ _______________

748. $\frac{4}{7} \div \frac{6}{7} =$ _______________

749. $\frac{8}{9} \div \frac{2}{12} =$ _______________

750. $\frac{1}{6} \div \frac{1}{3} =$ _______________

751. $\frac{2}{3} \div \frac{1}{4} =$ _______________

752. $\frac{1}{4} \div \frac{4}{8} =$ _______________

753. $\frac{1}{6} \div \frac{3}{10} =$ _______________

754. $\frac{2}{11} \div \frac{2}{3} =$ _______________

755. $\frac{3}{10} \div \frac{2}{4} =$ _______________

756. $\frac{7}{8} \div \frac{4}{7} =$ _______________

757. $\frac{3}{10} \div \frac{4}{5} =$ _______________

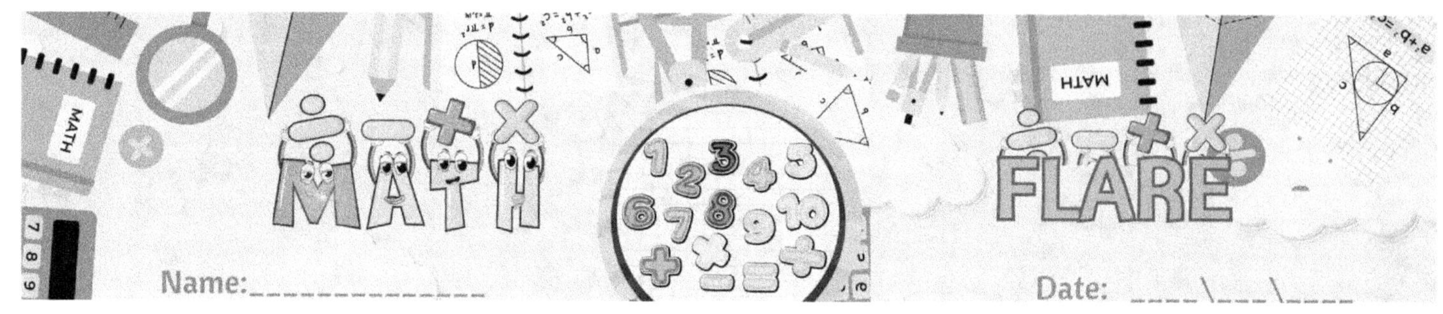

758. $\dfrac{1}{9} \div \dfrac{2}{3} =$ ______________

759. $\dfrac{1}{8} \div \dfrac{1}{8} =$ ______________

760. $\dfrac{3}{4} \div \dfrac{7}{11} =$ ______________

761. $\dfrac{3}{7} \div \dfrac{3}{7} =$ ______________

762. $\dfrac{1}{6} \div \dfrac{1}{8} =$ ______________

763. $\dfrac{1}{2} \div \dfrac{11}{12} =$ ______________

764. $\dfrac{3}{10} \div \dfrac{5}{11} =$ ______________

765. $\dfrac{8}{11} \div \dfrac{1}{5} =$ ______________

766. $\dfrac{2}{7} \div \dfrac{1}{3} =$ ______________

767. $\dfrac{1}{6} \div \dfrac{3}{9} =$ ______________

768. $\dfrac{2}{7} \div \dfrac{3}{8} =$ ______________

769. $\dfrac{8}{11} \div \dfrac{2}{11} =$ ______________

ANSWERS

Page 1:   Adding Decimals

1. 1,390.75	2. 1,382.77	3. 1,496.52	4. 1,029.48
5. 1,051.15	6. 1,053.23	7. 930.79	8. 875.38
9. 691.72	10. 517.99	11. 1,335.41	12. 1,380.03
13. 1,090.77	14. 1,090.95	15. 1,751.69	16. 1,453.38
17. 769.91	18. 1,477.34	19. 1,408.05	20. 1,039.20
21. 778.34	22. 377.74	23. 1,503.44	24. 1,331.85
25. 813.80	26. 559.51	27. 895.34	28. 1,103.27
29. 1,039.28	30. 1,375.27	31. 1,039.03	32. 1,685.32
33. 1,742.12	34. 1,540.40	35. 269.50	36. 849.69
37. 763.82	38. 1,470.52	39. 808.23	40. 628.24
41. 1,120.53	42. 1,144.23	43. 860.68	44. 702.97
45. 1,174.68	46. 1,194.88	47. 1,227.32	48. 1,882.93
49. 879.45	50. 979.66	51. 889.94	52. 1,115.51
53. 1,054.80	54. 511.69	55. 485.55	56. 1,796.54
57. 1,022.82	58. 323.59	59. 1,227.20	60. 1,170.26
61. 1,151.94	62. 778.14	63. 746.30	64. 1,061.76
65. 813.06	66. 1,191.17	67. 978.55	68. 1,070.47
69. 990.42	70. 1,192.36	71. 1,166.16	72. 728.27
73. 1,276.00	74. 1,134.15	75. 1,671.48	76. 1,379.67

77. 1,376.50   78. 896.59   79. 1,000.88   80. 1,426.27

81. 1,408.63   82. 686.27   83. 1,141.47   84. 1,402.49

85. 1,644.37   86. 1,242.64   87. 1,545.76   88. 1,298.09

89. 1,098.31   90. 1,920.91   91. 1,758.53   92. 1,297.23

93. 783.96   94. 1,084.92   95. 983.10   96. 740.62

97. 1,745.34   98. 1,181.61   99. 917.34   100. 1,000.55

Page 6: Subtracting Decimals

101. 237.93   102. 25.68   103. 191.79   104. 73.52   105. 347.33

106. 149.27   107. 268.37   108. 146.15   109. 653.28   110. 554.14

111. 179.80   112. 545.41   113. 619.55   114. 421.63   115. 116.67

116. 192.56   117. 353.12   118. 466.78   119. 402.79   120. 274.45

121. 115.89   122. 255.79   123. 276.44   124. 538.89   125. 331.22

126. 366.40   127. 764.72   128. 542.56   129. 457.07   130. 650.03

131. 780.03   132. 9.45   133. 631.21   134. 369.48   135. 76.22

136. 786.71   137. 172.20   138. 372.12   139. 322.59   140. 19.22

141. 59.04   142. 251.40   143. 215.12   144. 643.65   145. 257.49

146. 595.49   147. 135.90   148. 517.38   149. 112.22   150. 74.86

151. 90.02   152. 21.60   153. 515.95   154. 15.45   155. 62.74

156. 187.54   157. 459.66   158. 219.82   159. 89.45   160. 444.52

161. 509.51   162. 39.17   163. 94.83   164. 172.04   165. 218.08

166. 139.46   167. 331.18   168. 279.14   169. 166.36   170. 390.59

171. 49.34   172. 372.50   173. 11.65   174. 7.88   175. 196.77

176. 113.10   177. 423.51   178. 332.57   179. 419.83   180. 264.46

181. 129.08   182. 495.62   183. 751.71   184. 114.35   185. 357.49

186. 429.93   187. 31.03   188. 313.69   189. 454.05   190. 330.74

191. 59.99   192. 115.74   193. 25.34   194. 80.07   195. 176.97

196. 125.13   197. 126.40   198. 806.46   199. 300.31   200. 69.91

Page 11: Fraction Identification

201. 1/4   202. 2/5   203. 2/3   204. 3/4   205. 3/4   206. 7/10

207. 2/3   208. 7/8   209. 2/5   210. 1/3   211. 1/2   212. 1/5

213. 1/9   214. 11/16   215. 5/7   216. 2/5   217. 1/6   218. 2/3

219. 4/7   220. 1/8   221. 1/3   222. 2/9   223. 1/10   224. 11/12

225. 9/10   226. 1/7   227. 3/5   228. 8/9   229. 9/16   230. 1/4

231. 1/6   232. 1/8   233. 5/9   234. 1/4   235. 6/7   236. 4/15

237. 13/16   238. 1/2   239. 1/5   240. 1/3   241. 3/7   242. 3/16

243. 3/4   244. 2/7   245. 1/2   246. 1/2   247. 7/16   248. 13/15

249. 7/9   250. 3/8   251. 5/8   252. 3/8   253. 4/5   254. 1/3

255. 4/5   256. 11/15   257. 5/12   258. 3/4   259. 3/10   260. 5/6

261. 1/4   262. 1/2   263. 15/16   264. 1/5   265. 5/16   266. 1/12

267. 4/9   268. 4/5   269. 7/12   270. 14/15   271. 1/2   272. 2/3

273. 7/8   274. 1/15   275. 5/6   276. 2/3   277. 3/5   278. 2/15

279. 7/15   280. 1/16   281. 8/15   282. 5/8   283. 3/5   284. 1/2

285. 1/3   286. 1/2   287. 1/5   288. 4/9   289. 1/2   290. 1/2

291. 3/5   292. 1/2   293. 5/6   294. 3/4   295. 1/6

Page 23: Compare the Fractions

296. <   297. >   298. <   299. <   300. >   301. <   302. <   303. >

304. >   305. >   306. >   307. >   308. >   309. >   310. <   311. >

312. >   313. >   314. >   315. <   316. <   317. <   318. <   319. <

320. >   321. <   322. >   323. <   324. <   325. <   326. >   327. >

328. <   329. >   330. <   331. >   332. >   333. >   334. >   335. >

336. >   337. <   338. =   339. =   340. >   341. <   342. >   343. <

344. >   345. <   346. >   347. <   348. <   349. <   350. <   351. <

352. >   353. >   354. <   355. <   356. >   357. <   358. >   359. >

360. <   361. <   362. <   363. >   364. >   365. >   366. >   367. <

368. >   369. <   370. <   371. =   372. <   373. >   374. <   375. >

376. >   377. >   378. <   379. <   380. >   381. <   382. >   383. >

384. <   385. >   386. <   387. >   388. <   389. <   390. >   391. <

392. >   393. >   394. <   395. <   396. >   397. <   398. <   399. >

400. <   401. >   402. <   403. >

Page 32: Equivalent Fractions

404. 10   405. 8   406. 7   407. 70   408. 200   409. 144

410. 10   411. 10   412. 5   413. 11   414. 1   415. 8

416. 13   417. 16   418. 1   419. 2   420. 18   421. 13

422. 4   423. 3   424. 42   425. 99   426. 100   427. 2

428. 40   429. 28   430. 3   431. 15   432. 5   433. 90

434. 96   435. 1   436. 19   437. 18   438. 39   439. 6

440. 8   441. 18   442. 8   443. 49   444. 12   445. 16

446. 18   447. 1   448. 1   449. 2   450. 72   451. 27

452. 4   453. 20   454. 17   455. 14   456. 9   457. 13

458. 18   459. 22   460. 24   461. 1

Page 37: Fractions Addition: Common Denominator

462. 1/1   463. 2/7   464. 1/4   465. 5/6   466. 2/3   467. 3/4

468. 3/11   469. 2/3   470. 3/4   471. 1/2   472. 4/5   473. 2/5

474. 7/12   475. 8/9   476. 5/7   477. 8/11   478. 3/5   479. 1/2

480. 7/8   481. 1/2   482. 1/5   483. 8/9   484. 3/4   485. 10/11

486. 3/4   487. 3/4   488. 2/3   489. 4/7   490. 4/5   491. 6/7

492. 5/8   493. 1/3   494. 5/6   495. 9/10   496. 5/11   497. 7/9

498. 9/10   499. 5/6   500. 3/5   501. 9/11   502. 5/8   503. 7/12

504. 9/11   505. 5/7   506. 2/3   507. 2/3   508. 7/10   509. 6/7

510. 2/3   511. 8/11   512. 11/12   513. 4/5   514. 2/9   515. 5/8

516. 2/3   517. 3/5   518. 3/7   519. 3/4   520. 2/3   521. 3/5

522. 3/10   523. 2/3   524. 6/11   525. 5/6   526. 7/11   527. 7/9

528. 7/12   529. 3/7   530. 3/4   531. 1/2   532. 3/5   533. 2/3

534. 7/9   535. 3/8   536. 9/11   537. 7/10   538. 5/8   539. 2/3

540. 5/6   541. 8/9   542. 6/11   543. 5/9   544. 1/2   545. 9/11

546. 5/6   547. 7/10   548. 7/9   549. 5/11   550. 1/2   551. 3/4

552. 5/6   553. 8/11   554. 5/7   555. 4/9   556. 2/3   557. 11/12

Page 44:   Fractions Subtraction - Common Denominator

558. 1/3   559. 5/12   560. 5/11   561. 2/9   562. 1/5   563. 1/8

564. 1/7   565. 1/2   566. 1/5   567. 1/5   568. 1/2   569. 1/3

570. 2/11   571. 4/9   572. 1/11   573. 1/4   574. 1/6   575. 1/10

576. 2/9   577. 2/5   578. 1/12   579. 3/7   580. 1/2   581. 1/5

582. 1/6   583. 2/3   584. 2/7   585. 1/5   586. 1/11   587. 1/9

588. 3/7   589. 1/10   590. 1/4   591. 1/3   592. 1/4   593. 1/2

594. 1/4   595. 1/3   596. 5/9   597. 1/7   598. 3/10   599. 1/11

600. 3/8   601. 2/11   602. 4/9   603. 3/10   604. 1/4   605. 1/8

606. 1/6   607. 1/7   608. 1/3   609. 1/2   610. 1/4   611. 2/3

612. 1/7   613. 1/2   614. 1/3   615. 2/7   616. 3/10   617. 3/11

618. 7/12   619. 3/5   620. 4/5   621. 3/11   622. 1/2   623. 1/12

624. 2/11   625. 1/5   626. 3/11   627. 4/7   628. 1/4   629. 3/10

630. 7/9   631. 3/4   632. 1/3   633. 1/9   634. 4/11   635. 1/6

636. 2/9   637. 3/11   638. 1/2   639. 1/6   640. 1/11   641. 1/10

642. 1/2   643. 1/2   644. 1/9   645. 4/7   646. 1/12   647. 1/10

648. 3/11   649. 2/9   650. 1/12   651. 3/8   652. 1/5   653. 1/2

Page 51:   Fractions Multiplication

654. 21/40	655. 3/8	656. 5/21	657. 4/77	658. 63/88
659. 4/9	660. 2/5	661. 5/12	662. 4/15	663. 20/33
664. 3/28	665. 5/9	666. 7/18	667. 1/5	668. 1/24
669. 5/12	670. 7/15	671. 2/55	672. 1/14	673. 3/7
674. 5/18	675. 27/55	676. 8/15	677. 1/11	678. 1/5
679. 5/28	680. 3/16	681. 5/18	682. 1/3	683. 1/2
684. 5/21	685. 12/35	686. 1/4	687. 3/22	688. 3/5
689. 14/27	690. 7/96	691. 3/14	692. 1/9	693. 14/55
694. 1/14	695. 1/12	696. 3/10	697. 10/33	698. 1/6
699. 4/27	700. 25/44	701. 35/88	702. 11/30	703. 1/14
704. 1/3	705. 3/8	706. 9/77	707. 27/40	708. 5/12
709. 1/4	710. 3/35	711. 63/80		

Page 56:   Fractions Division

712. 1/3	713. 1 13/14	714. 1/6	715. 2 8/11	716. 1
717. 1 5/72	718. 7/15	719. 1 13/27	720. 3 3/8	721. 2 7/10
722. 77/96	723. 20/21	724. 2	725. 1 1/5	726. 1 1/2
727. 7/48	728. 60/77	729. 1 1/5	730. 8 2/11	731. 24/35
732. 6/7	733. 3 1/3	734. 1 7/9	735. 7 1/2	736. 1 1/3
737. 2/3	738. 11/14	739. 1/4	740. 1 1/5	741. 8/11
742. 1 17/18	743. 4/5	744. 15/16	745. 1/6	746. 77/90

747. 9/20   748. 2/3   749. 5 1/3   750. 1/2   751. 2 2/3

752. 1/2   753. 5/9   754. 3/11   755. 3/5   756. 1 17/32

757. 3/8   758. 1/6   759. 1   760. 1 5/28   761. 1

762. 1 1/3   763. 6/11   764. 33/50   765. 3 7/11   766. 6/7

767. 1/2   768. 16/21   769. 4